WOMEN'S
VISIONS

Edited by Ofelia Ortega

WOMEN'S VISIONS

Theological Reflection, Celebration, Action

WCC Publications, Geneva

Cover design: Edwin Hassink
Cover photo: TIB

ISBN 2-8254-1144-2

Printed in Switzerland

Table of Contents

Introduction

Women... no longer silent,
No longer silenced.
Women speaking out from the depth of our pain,
Challenging traditional understandings of society,
of the church, of community, of our faith...

Women demanding a just world.
A world without war and conflict,
A violence-free world.
A world without racism/casteism, and no xenophobia,
With no discrimination, no alienation,
No exclusion, no homophobia.
A world of playfulness, of laughter,
of safety for all children,
A world where all will have enough
and no one will have too much,
A world where people and creation
will live in harmony,
A world where caring, nurturing
and loving become the norm,
A world where each has the space
For their own creativity, their own choices,
Finding their selfhood, their dignity in community.

Women in dialogue:
Women — shifting paradigms, moving into new realms.
Women — transforming, reconstructing, recreating.

Women — forging strong links of solidarity,
Affirming our diversity,
Discovering commonalities,
Hoping... dreaming... visioning,
re-imagining... longing
And... struggling...
For a new society, a new church, a new world.

The Ecumenical Decade: Churches in Solidarity with Women,
Can 2000 years of patriarchal history be erased
In just ten years?
The challenge to the churches is to
"Take back the Decade" and to make it...
A Decade of solidarity with women!
A Decade ushering in change!
Listening to the voices of women!

Women's theological voices are emerging in every continent of the world. New theological visions are being born out of the womb of women's experiences of suffering, pain and struggles. Women's voices point to the celebratory, the life-giving and life-protecting. Emerging feminist theological methodologies draw strength from the intuitive, the poetic, the lyrical. Women all over the world recognize that traditional expectations of long-suffering and sacrifice which have been imposed on women can no longer be accepted. Women affirm theologies of hope and action, of laughter and joy, of liberation and freedom for all God's people and all creation.

This was the spirit that flowed over the seminar "Women in Dialogue: Wholeness of Vision towards the 21st Century", held in Bossey, outside Geneva, from 29 April to 8 May 1994. The seminar was organized by the Ecumenical Institute in Bossey, along with the women's programmes of the World Council of Churches, World Alliance of Reformed Churches, Lutheran World Federation and Conference of European Churches, as a contribution to the process of marking the midpoint of the Ecumenical Decade — Churches in Solidarity with Women (1988-1998). The essays in this book are drawn from the presentations made at this seminar.

The seminar took its place in a tradition that was inaugurated in 1985 with a joint venture between the Ecumenical Institute and the women's programmes of the four international church organizations headquartered in the Ecumenical Centre in Geneva. This book can thus be seen as the culmination of almost ten years of women's seminars dealing with a variety of topics, responding not only to the specific programmatic emphases of the Ecumenical Decade but also to the needs of those churches and ecumenical bodies that are trying to build up the community of women and men in church and society.

Themes such as Women in Church Leadership, New Reading of the Bible, Women's Spirituality, Women and Economic Development, Challenges Facing Young Women Theologians, Models of Renewed Community, Women and Liturgy, and Feminist Images in Orthodox Spirituality have featured in our theological reflection, as we have sought strategies to strengthen women's participation in our communities. We have made great efforts not only to challenge rigid structures but to pursue serious research in theological reflection, biblical hermeneutics and creative liturgical experiences.

Together we have sought the "good odour of life — where the flowers of many colours are growing, not only one colour but many colours; where we can listen to many sounds, not only one; where we can dialogue with many traditions, not only one; where we can dance and break down the great walls that do not allow dance, to expose ourselves to the Wind, to the Spirit that ruffles our hair and our lives".[1]

The regional presentations of the May 1994 seminar reflected present trends in women's theological work and the variety of methodologies that women are using. For women, this diversity of theologies and methodologies is the key to any real dialogue. Diversity was affirmed because at the heart of the new theological movement is the common search for justice and dignity for all women and for all people.

To be sure, this rich diversity could be represented only incompletely at the seminar in Bossey and thus in this book. In particular, we regret that it has not been possible to include an account of recent developments in women's theology in Central and Eastern Europe.

Women recognize the need for more intentional interaction between women in academia and women activists as well as women at the grassroots in the development of theology, because theology comes out of the lived experiences of women. The contributions of indigenous women and black women were highlighted as being important in this. As one group at the seminar described it, "theology is not separated from life but is a part of it. Becoming a feminist theologian requires getting involved in the struggles for life." Another group saw "the power of women from popular movements, the growing awareness of the role of religion in women's lives, the spirituality of women's daily lives and the moving of women from being victims to survivors and on to becoming agents of change" as resources in bridging the gaps between women.

Patriarchy and patriarchal violence are at the heart of the concern that has urged women on to reconstruct basic theological affirmations. Linked with global economic injustice that has systematically marginalized and destroyed the life and livelihood of millions of people, particularly women and children, patriarchy has been a formidable force silencing women and rendering them invisible in all spheres of life.

Women in theology see the urgency of the "dialogue of cultures". On the one hand, the liberation potential within all cultures needs to be asserted, because the dominant Western culture has so often attempted to suppress cultures and impose values and ways of life on peoples of the South. However, as women we recognize that all cultures perpetuate certain patriarchal institutions of discrimination against women. Women see the need for the transformation of cultures, challenged by the gospel, so that cultural hermeneutics can become an interpretative tool for women in their feminist theological search.

The violence women experience, not only in society and on the streets but also in what one might hope would be safer spheres — the home and the church — has been central to recent theological work by women. This has led to an exploration of some basic theological affirmations, including the concept of sacrifice and the significance of the cross, the concept of salvation and atonement, the church's insistence on forgiveness as a virtue. To women who have been immersed in a theology of self-sacrifice, denying themselves value and dignity, the need is for a theology of liberation and celebration of women's lives.

In this context, women have begun exposing the silence that shrouds any discussions on human sexuality and the consequent reluctance to engage such ethical issues as abortion and the use of contraceptives, as well as the exclusion of gays and lesbians from church life. Women celebrate their sexuality and affirm that understanding human sexuality is integral to our self-understanding as women and that women have a key role to play in making the church into a more inclusive and caring community.

The hope is for a new church — a church responsive to the new theological visions of women as they identify the urgent issues that need to be addressed. The Ecumenical Decade provides a platform for commitment and action on the part of the churches. Can women turn to the church for solidarity? Can this be a time for the churches to recognize women's longings for a just and violence-free world?

As the final statement of the seminar describes it:

> We have gathered as women to envision a just future in church and society, for women, for children and for men. Much threatens such a future. To create it will be hard work. For the majority of women on earth, this is first of all the hard work of survival.

We have gathered to begin envisioning the 21st century,
> by letting the light of our lives' stories shine,
> even with the fires of tribulation;
> by celebrating our diversity and honouring our differences,
> even when they lead to conflict; and
> by committing ourselves to act together for a just future,
> even when we are divided by economic, political,
> cultural and religious structures and beliefs.

We are united
> by our solemn rejection of the pervasive, growing violence
> against women in the whole world;
> by our hope in the freedom born of faith
> in Mary's son, Jesus; and
> by our desire for a new, whole community of human beings,
> earth and all creatures, within the embrace of God.

This seminar helped us to sum up our "visions and dreams", recovering and rebuilding our past memories, being critical of the present and opening new ways into the future. Our hope is that the collection of essays here will help to engage many more people — women and men — in that process of theological reflection, celebration and action.

Ofelia Ortega, Ecumenical Institute, WCC
Aruna Gnanadason, Women's Programme, WCC
Musimbi Kanyoro, Lutheran World Federation
Nyambura Njoroge, World Alliance of Reformed Churches
Irja Askola, Conference of European Churches
Beate Stierle, Ecumenical Institute, WCC

NOTE

[1] Ivone Gebara, "Mujer e Iglesia en America Latina: 500 Años Después", in *Aportes para una Teología Feminista*, Santiago de Chile, Ediciones Revue, Vol. 3, No. 6, September 1993, p.131.

Theology from the Perspective of African Women

ELIZABETH AMOAH

Theology from the perspective of African women should not be seen only in terms of what is done in academic institutions. Within the African context, theology is done at all levels by different categories of women. African women who are not formally educated express their theology in the spontaneous, poetic lyrics, songs and prayers which are an ordinary part of their everyday lives. In the African instituted churches, women freely involve themselves in preaching, prophesying, healing and counselling. At a more formal level one can cite examples of women Sunday school teachers and guidance counsellors for children in the churches. All these activities involve genuine theologizing by women; that is, they involve reflections on and conceptions of God in their daily lives and needs and in the church.

At the academic level a number of African women have consistently over the past 15 years done writing and research on theological issues, thus contributing to the fund of theological knowledge. African women in theology stress the experiences of women as one of the bases for theologizing. While they accept African culture as a basis for theology, they go on to demand a critique of African culture. This critical stance is extended to the unquestioning use of the Bible as the source of theology. Such a methodology is very evident in the works of the Circle of Concerned African Women in Theology. Many of the women in this group recognize the dehumanizing effects, especially on women, of certain aspects of African beliefs and practices. Such persistent customs as widowhood rituals, food taboos, traditional laws on inheritance and female circumcision impinge on the health and rights of women.

At the same time, African women in theology are involved in the struggles of their male counterparts and share some common concerns with them. Indeed, African women experience the effects of racism, poverty, social, economic and political problems, which have resulted in ethnic wars, even more than their male counterparts. Such pressing issues also form the content of African women's theology.

Within this framework, I would identify two basic aspects of African women's theological reflections:

First, their critique is directed at the very basis of the whole of orthodox theological thinking. God as creator is indeed the source of all things, and all humanity is endowed with equal capabilities. In God's mercy, all humanity shares equally in the common wealth given by God. In other words, wherever God is, be it in the church, in the home, in the society, no system should be used to dehumanize and marginalize anyone on the basis of gender, race, colour and class. No form of discrimination among the creatures of God can ever be justifiable.

Such a contention is crucial, as it emphasizes integrity and equality as fundamental and formative principles of creation. This principle underlies the traditional African affirmation expressed in the proverb of the Akan people (who comprise many ethnic groups in southern Ghana): *Onipa nyinaa ye Onyame mma, obi nnye Asaase ba* — all human beings are children of God, no one is the child of the earth. Humanity has the image of God and thus each and every human being, regardless of age, class, gender or race, is endowed with dignity and respect. Physical, spiritual, social, economic and cultural resources should be used to sustain all God's creatures. This is in line with the message of Jesus Christ, who came to give abundant life to all. African women therefore see Christ as the Saviour who takes them out of all life-denying situations and gives them back the abundant life.

Second, the church is seen as the community of women and men who believe in God the creator and giver of abundant life, integrity and respect to all. The church as an institution cannot escape criticism when its action goes against this fundamental law of enhancing and preserving the equality and integrity of all creatures. In other words, both the church's activities and its structural organization should evince this principle of essential unity and equality. In particular, the church should encourage and allow women to fulfil their callings and responsibilities as equal inheritors of the common wealth of God.

A fundamental emphasis in the theology of many African women is thus inclusiveness, the insistence that women and men, Christians and people of other faiths are all part of a community fighting for survival and a nobler social and religious life. If our theology is eventually to remove all the things which create hardship, it should be for the good of all.

African feminist ecclesiology

Any discussion of the church in Africa as an institution should start from the basic observation of the numerical preponderance of women in all the churches, both African instituted churches and those established by the Western missionaries over a century ago. Whether these women who are always seen in church buildings and gatherings in their numbers have a voice in the church is quite another issue. They are really the pillars of the church but they are silent ones.

The presence of the silent majority of women in the hierarchical structures of many churches in Africa is a shameful contradiction of the Christian faith. Theologically, the church is a chosen community and a gift of God. In this community all people, women and men, young and old, should feel very much at home as equal creatures of God. All the members of the church — the whole fellowship of believers — share a common service of witnessing to the love of God in Jesus Christ and building koinonia. At the same time, the diversity of talents and gifts in the church should be affirmed, and there is a need to emphasize that all in this community are empowered through the Holy Spirit to use their diverse gifts to participate equally, to share in and to build the church as the community of the people of God.

Despite this ideal, it is the considered view of many African women that the organization of the church has reflected a predominantly male bias in its structure and in its process of decision-making. Some attempts have been made to modify this general situation, but much remains to be done.

An instructive example is the ordination of women in many African churches of Western missionary origin. It is difficult to avoid the suspicion that this tends to be merely decorative, as if women are ordained to satisfy some emergent trend. By contrast, one may point to the situation of women in the African instituted churches. Here authority seems more centred on the Holy Spirit and charisma, and women in general are not excluded from important offices and positions. They freely perform their roles as pastors, healers and prophetesses.

It is therefore no wonder that many of the ecclesiological writings of African women begin by criticizing and condemning the church for failing in its essential call to be the community of the people of God and the "salt of the earth". At the same time, some women are doing research and writing about the lives and activities of women in the African instituted churches, some of which are founded and organized by women. The ultimate aim is to find new models of women's approach to ministry.

Clearly, one mission of the church is to teach its members and to prepare them for the ministry. In this respect, much remains to be done with reference to women in theological education in Africa. Many more men than women are enrolled in the African theological institutions, with the average ratio of female students to male students being one to six. At higher levels of teaching and research the situation is not very different. Trinity College in Legon, an ecumenical theological institute, has for a long time had no woman faculty member.

Given these shortcomings, church women in Africa are increasingly forming solidarity groups to address the special needs of women. The many women's fellowships in the church are strengthening themselves and organizing their own missions — "adopting" hospital wards for women, helping women in refugee situations, counselling and caring for AIDS patients, working with prostitutes and the like. Women in the Presbyterian Church of Kenya have organized themselves to fight against female circumcision. Similarly, women in the Presbyterian Church of Ghana, in collaboration with other church women, have organized series of seminars on widowhood rituals and are pressing the church authorities for laws against such practices. Some women's groups are organizing and setting up vocational training schemes for women in rural areas in small-scale industries such as food processing, tie and dye making. The Ecumenical Decade of the Churches in Solidarity with Women is encouraging women to do more of these sorts of things.

Women in the church in Africa have great influence on worship. Women's groups feature in church services, especially choirs and bands, and in the African instituted churches as healers and prophetesses. Such involvements give women visibility, but again, when it comes to structures related to decision-making, they become invisible.

Four challenges emerge from the general situation of women in the churches of Africa:

1. Church women should vigorously continue to explore further avenues for solving the problems facing women. For example, they should team up to impress upon all members of the church the need to be concerned with some of the resistant traditions, customs and practices which adversely affect women, such as widowhood rituals and customs relating to inheritance. They should continue to press church leaders to formulate laws against such practices.

2. The actual impact of ordained women in Africa should be assessed. Such exploration should include their role, the images the public has of them, their family lives and the factors that hinder or promote their

effectiveness. Already a member of the Circle of Concerned African Women in Theology is doing research on women pastors in the Anglican Church in Uganda for a doctoral programme.

3. It is urgent to press the church authorities to improve female theological education and remove all obstacles in the way of this, including the shortage of employment possibilities for theologically educated women which make effective use of their education and gifts.

4. Ordained and lay women should come together for discussions of how they see their roles as women in the church. In other words, they should find new ways to project the feminist approach to ministry.

Women's theology groups

The Circle of Concerned African Women in Theology grew out of the decision by the Ecumenical Association of Third World Theologians (EATWOT) at its 1988 meeting to appoint conveners for women's theology groups in each region of the world. The African women of EATWOT decided to form a biennial institute for women in religion and culture, an area in which they saw promise for creating a liberative theology that would respond to their needs.

An initial convocation, under the theme "Daughters of Africa, Arise!", was convened in Accra, Ghana, in September 1989. Workshops were held at which papers were read and discussed. Ghanaian church women followed the meeting day by day. Coordinators for the various zones were selected, and they set up national and zonal meetings in their parts of the continent. These coordinators have met in Nairobi in 1990 and again in 1992 to assess the progress and prospects of women theologians in Africa. Subsequently, three conferences were planned for English-speaking West Africa (1993), Eastern and Southern Africa (1994) and French-speaking West and Central Africa (1995).

An idea of the work of the Circle can be seen in the following excerpts from reports of two chapters, on South Africa and East Africa.

• Most of those attending the launch of the Cape Town chapter of the Circle in March 1993 were men. While Cape Town has three universities with departments of religious studies and theology, there is only one woman lecturer, Denise Ackermann. The male lecturers in religious studies at the University of Cape Town were supportive, and the head of the department suggested broadening the original invitation to include all interested people in the area.

The group is now a multi-racial one and its scope has widened beyond Cape Town through the participation of students from other parts of South

Africa as well as Lesotho and Malawi. What binds the group together, says Sister Irene Matsoso, is "our faith in a higher being that we call different names, and our hurts from our religious cultures as a result of being women".

An immediate priority is raising funds from Christian and Muslim sources to establish a post for a woman theologian at UCT, to help ensure continuation of the Circle as students come and go. The hope is that once the post is set up, the university will take it over. Another project is that of the members' writing their own theological stories for eventual publication.

To keep the vision alive, the group has covenanted to meet one Saturday a month. The success of the launch surprised the participants, and most members feel that the Circle came at just the right time to meet the need for a forum in which women in theology could meet. At the same time, it offered a much-needed sense of sisterhood for facing common problems, tapping each other's resources to reflect on their lives from a woman's point of view.

• The East African Circle defines itself as "a group of Christian women theologians who are concerned with the issues of human liberation in all its dimensions". That vision is broken down into a five-fold task:

1)   to share our awareness and concern for the need for human liberation;
2)   to create a context in which this awareness and concern can be nurtured and developed;
3)   to redefine ourselves in the light of this insight and consciousness;
4)   to unmask and name those aspects of our social structures which are oppressive or life-denying to some people and seek their replacement with liberative ones;
5)   to initiate an atmosphere and create a forum within which women's experiences and stories can be articulated and written in order to contribute to the forming and shaping of human consciousness.

The Circle believes that its work will have the following effects:

1)   People will become more sensitive to and conscious of the subtle ways in which society discriminates against certain groups of people, particularly women, so that they join in the struggle of eliminating these social evils.
2)   Those who are victims of oppressive and exploitative structures will begin to appreciate themselves, love themselves, affirm themselves

and actualize their God-given gifts in order to contribute more to
society.
3) Society will become a context in which all find personal and communal fulfilment.

This is a task, the group believes, which can be started in each
individual's life situation, whether at home as a housewife or at the place
of work as teacher, pastor, lawyer, nurse or other, and gradually be
expanded to embrace as many contexts as possible. The overall goal and
vision is "the recapturing of the Christian vision of humanity and human
relations as inaugurated by Jesus".

Beyond abstractions
One of the basic challenges for women in theology (especially those
in an academic context) is to ensure that their theological thinking is
oriented not only to the academic world but also to ordinary women
struggling daily for survival. There is a need to go to these women to
know their spiritual and social needs and to reflect with them. This is all
the more important because of the political and ideological connotations
that the term "feminism" has among many ordinary African women, who
see it as something for a small class of women who are merely struggling
against male domination and are saying many abstract things that are
meaningless to their ordinary daily life.

African women in theology must open up their discussion to include
issues arising from contemporary social and economic systems which
result in the poverty and the death of many Africans. This concern for
contemporary issues is all the more important because traditional African
societies are themselves undergoing rapid change in almost every sector.
Issues such as the effects on women of structural adjustment programmes,
environmental degradation and international trade systems need to be high
on the agenda of women in theology, as well as the struggle for democrati-
zation in many African societies and, most recently, the brutal massacre of
helpless women, children and men in Rwanda, Burundi and elsewhere.
Again, it is women and children who bear the brunt of such situations.
African women should, through their theologies, be able to make their
governments aware of the sanctity and preciousness of human life.

A final challenge is to fight for the training of many more women who
can help in effective theologizing.

All of this requires extensive human and material resources, underlin-
ing the need for efficient and generous sharing.

Challenges for Feminist Theology in Francophone Africa

MARGUÉRITE FASSINOU

Texts from Francophone Africa expressing feminist points of view in theology have not been widely published and are therefore little known. Feminist theology is advancing slowly but surely in our sub-region, but if feminist theology is understood as "a new way of doing theology, that is, of reading and listening to God's Word in revelation and then rewriting the interpretation of that Word for the church, in a rereading that will be different from that of tradition, hitherto monopolized by men",[1] then a great deal remains to be done here, as in most African countries.

Feminist theology in our sub-region is a practical exercise. Women wage a daily struggle for integration into the church to make it an inclusive Christian community in which all members without discrimination will feel themselves as children of God and there will be no obstacles preventing women from entering the ordained ministry. In the present cultural context, however, women are still regarded as inferior to men in both society and the church; indeed, society is ahead of the church in recognizing and implementing women's rights.

What is needed is a movement of renewal in the Christian community, which often clings desperately to outdated traditions devoid of any solid theological basis. Such winds of change are blowing at present in almost all the churches, just as the winds of democracy are sweeping through society. I shall focus on four areas in which God's people might address particular challenges in the area of feminist theology in our sub-region, drawing especially on experiences in my own country, Benin.

1. The struggle for access for women to theological education and the ordained ministry in all Christian communities and encouragement of more vocations to the ministry among women where this is already recognized.

2. Intensive evangelism among families and especially among women and young people.
3. Continued work on the inculturation of the gospel, so that it can be spread more widely and save women from the negative aspects of their cultures.
4. The fight against social injustice, the economic and political crisis, poverty and misery.

Theological training and the ministry

The majority of churches in Francophone Africa do not yet admit women either to theological training or to the ordained ministry. The doors of a few training institutions have been opened to them only in the last few years. The School of Theology in Porto Novo, Benin, for instance, established in 1926, did not admit a woman student until 1982. Similarly, the Faculty of Theology in Yaoundé, Cameroon, had no women students for a long time.

Two thousand years ago Jesus Christ gave women their rightful place despite the heavy yoke of the Jewish culture weighing on them. For women in general and Jewish women in particular the coming of Jesus meant a revolution. This revolution must continue. It is essential that women should know more about God's word and be able to study it systematically. This is one means for the struggle to make the liberation granted to all women and men a living reality and to open the eyes of our sisters who, through ignorance, still acquiesce in their own oppression and exploitation.

Feminist theology would be an empty notion if there were no women theologians. Women's lack of enthusiasm for theological studies may stem from either the constraints of the ordained ministry or the sexual discrimination displayed by both church members and church authorities.

For example, a layman in my church was assisting a woman minister in leading a worship service not long ago. Even before it started, annoyed that she had not asked him to take certain parts of the service, he complained that she was too authoritarian. At the end of the service, the lay preacher, enraged that the woman minister had not asked him to lead the closing prayer with the choir, seized her by the collar and began to threaten her. Members of the congregation had to intervene to put an end to this sorry spectacle. Certainly he would not have behaved like this if the pastor had been a man. Although he was consequently suspended, the harm has been done, for he had already undermined the minister's authority. I believe that the more women ministers there are, the fewer incidents of this kind will happen, for women in the ministry will have had time to assert themselves both by their numbers and by the quality of their work.

African Christian leaders should not try to prevent the entry of women into the ordained ministry. They need only look objectively at our traditional religions to see the place occupied by women there as priestesses and teachers of spirituality. We should have the courage to learn some lessons from the cult of *vodun*, because not everything in it is satanical.

Evangelism for all, especially women

Evangelism, the church's primary task, is an urgent need in many of our countries. Here I shall focus on Benin, where the coming of democracy has permitted a new flowering of culture. Some years ago, the "Ouidah 92" festival celebrated fellowship between African Americans and Africans in the arts and *vodun* worship. Such impressive cultural events have led us to discover Benin as the cradle and world capital of *vodun*.

This cult, with its multitude of divinities, shrivelled to almost nothing under the previous Marxist-Leninist political regime. Now it has regained its status and has a well-structured organization from the local to the national level. As an element of our cultural heritage, *vodun* is sometimes glorified by political authorities, and a national *vodun* day has even been mooted. Abandoned convents which were falling into ruin have been restored to life thanks to recruitment and the enclosure of new adepts, among them many women, girls and children of a very young age.

In 1992 I carried out a study on the place and role of children and women in the different *vodun* cults for a national consultation on "Traditional Religion — Democracy and Development". The findings of this research showed me the importance of women in this cult.

The 1992 national census disclosed that more than one-third of Benin's 4.9 million people practise the traditional religions. More women practise *vodun* than belong to all Christian denominations together, Protestant and Catholic. For this reason alone it is urgent that we evangelize families, especially the girls and women, who are the backbone of any society. Being a Christian cannot mean relinquishing our culture; we must remain genuinely African while still being good Christian men and women. A Chinese proverb says that "to educate a man is to educate an individual, but to educate a woman is to educate a nation". The same is true in religion: to evangelize women is to bring the family and hence the nation to Christ.

Abigaël, a lovely young women from the village of Dékanmè, was converted to Christianity some decades ago when she was living in the town with her guardians. When she returned to her village, her father, a *vodun* adept, disregarding his daughter's faith, married her to the chief of a *vodun* convent. Out of obedience she joined her husband's household but, determined to resist to the end, Abigaël continued to read her Bible, to give praise and to lead a life of prayer.

She refused to share her husband's bed; and to make sure she would not be poisoned or bewitched, she ate only food she had prepared herself. She remained adamant for a long time. Every time her husband desired her, she insisted that he adopt the Christian faith before she would give herself to him. As she was very beautiful her husband finally agreed to become Christian despite his being the head of a convent. His conversion was soon followed by that of the *vodunsi*, which inevitably aroused the anger of the other adepts of the cult in the village. This young woman gradually succeeded in bringing several other villagers to Christ and teaching them to read the Bible.

One day, one of her step-nieces whom she had converted to Christianity was abducted and taken to the *vodun* convent by relatives. Angered, Abigaël forced her way into the convent, found the girl, removed all the necklaces and clothes she was wearing as a new recruit and took her away. On top of everything else Abigaël had done, this sacrilege was too much for the *vodun* worshippers, and so they decided she must die following a ritual ceremony of imprecation called *Oman*. Her death warrant was signed and the days of the ceremony fixed.

The day before they were due to begin, the grand *vodunnon*, who was supposed to preside over the ritual, died mysteriously exactly at midday, to the great surprise of all the *vodun* adepts. Chaos and general panic ensued. Several *vodunnon* went to see Abigaël in secret to get to know more about the God she worshipped, who was so powerful. Most of them subsequently converted in order to place themselves under the protection of this great God who was more powerful than their gods. The planned *Oman* ceremony never took place.

This woman who was determined to fight to the end against the forces of the adversary had the victory thanks to the God of Jesus Christ under whose protection she lived. Thus Abigaël served as an instrument of evangelism, and almost the whole village of Dékanmè was converted to Christianity.

Let me tell you about another case of resistance by a woman from early 1994. With the resurgence of the activities of the *vodun* cult, new adepts are frequently recruited. Each divinity has a number of families who periodically supply them with followers, and so it came to the turn of the father of one family to fulfil this duty by giving one of his children. He selected one of his daughters and gave her name to the *vodunnon*. When she was informed of this she fled from her father's house and hid. On the day of the recruitment the assistants of the *vodunnon* decided to take one of the missing girl's sisters instead. Although this girl was a Christian and was learning the catechism, she was taken to the convent.

She reacted by going on a hunger strike. The leader of the convent, afraid that she might die, went to her father after several days and asked him to come and take her away. But the father, fearing reprisal from the *vodunnon*, went instead to the police to help to get her out. The police officers demanded that the leaders of the convent guarantee that nothing would happen to the girl. They complied. So the girl regained her freedom and returned to the church as before.

Making women the target of evangelism is a good method because the determination and spiritual strength of women have a great impact when it comes to transforming the milieu in which they live, in both spiritual and material terms.

The young girl and Abigaël are still alive today. Like the Canaanite woman, the latter played the part of an apostle in her village, where she led many souls to Christ. A deep faith, a life of prayer and fasting and effective practice of Christian ethics are needed to cope with the situations which these two Christian women victoriously surmounted. "For our struggle is not against enemies of blood and flesh, but against the rulers, against the authorities, against the cosmic powers of this present darkness... Therefore take up the whole armour of God, so that you may be able to withstand on that evil day, and having done everything to stand firm" (Eph. 6:12-13).

It is clearly essential for members of the church to be thoroughly evangelized themselves before reaching out to others. God is always at work, and Christianity can and must impose respect in situations where it is challenged by adepts of other religions. And in this, women — like Deborah, Lydia, Priscilla and many others in the Bible — are effective instruments in the hand of God. They are the apostles who without bearing the name were and still are at work in the Lord's field.

Inculturation of the gospel

The gospel needs to become part of the culture in order that it can be more easily understood and practised in any given milieu. Expressed solely in terms of a foreign culture, as it was in the early days of the missionary era, the good news cannot bring liberation to the believers for whom it is intended, especially when they are women and, as is often the case, victims of the negative aspects of social customs governing widowhood, levirate marriage, arranged marriage and the right to inherit property.

All cultures are enhanced in the light of the gospel, and their unique and positive aspects are restored to their proper value. The church can be a driving force in defending Africa's cultural identities. But we urgently need to do more to contextualize the expression of our faith in liturgy, moments of special celebration like birth, marriage and death, literature and the arts, healing through prayer and traditional medicines. Some churches have gone a long way in their attempts at contextualization, but others still seem bent on stripping their spiritual and community practice of any cultural marks. For example, one Christian community has suppressed the service on the eighth day after the birth of a child. By contrast, I was pleasantly surprised at a recent house-blessing service conducted by Methodist pastors at Badagry in Nigeria. During the prayer, the pastor conducting the service first scattered salt over the floor of the house (symbol of conservation), then did the same with water (symbol of life), then invited everyone else to do so. These gestures are linked with African philosophy and are in no way anti-evangelical.

Among the traditions which enslave African women are customs concerning widowhood and levirate marriage which are still very much alive in both the towns and the countryside. The widow's social class can alleviate some of the effects, but certain constraints persist: not getting up every day, not going out during the first months, sometimes sleeping on the ground, weeping at given times. One of the corollaries of widowhood is levirate marriage, justified by the need to keep the deceased husband's belongings in his family. Girls are prevented from inheriting their parents' property for similar reasons.

A familiar Old Testament story of levirate marriage tells of two Moabite women, Orpah and Ruth, the widows of two brothers from a family in Bethlehem who had gone to Moab during a famine. When their father-in-law died, their mother-in-law Naomi wanted to return to her own country, and she told Orpah and Ruth to return to their families. Orpah agreed, but Ruth chose to follow Naomi. Later she married Boaz, relative of her dead father-in-law, as the result of a stratagem organized by Naomi. The child born of this union was an ancestor of Jesus Christ.

This story could serve to illustrate the two possibilities that should be offered to widows in Africa. Orpah and Ruth were free to return to their respective families; in other words, they were free to remarry without constraint. Orpah chose to take that freedom; Ruth remained with her mother-in-law, which took her into a levirate marriage with a kinsman of her husband.

The practice of levirate marriage continues to put many widows in Africa, especially young women, in a very difficult position. There are even cases of killing widows who resist it. Let me give an example in which the victim was one of my own sisters.

K.B. married a man who became prosperous after their marriage. The two of them lived together happily, and five children were born of their union. Then the husband was killed in a road accident. After the ceremonies of widowhood were completed, K.B.'s life returned to normal until the older brother of her deceased husband, a man who had lost everything, sought to marry her under the custom of levirate, so that he could control the possessions left by his younger brother. K.B. was unwilling, and refused.

Without her knowledge, her brother-in-law tried, though unsuccessfully, to sell the house she and her children lived in. Then she fell mysteriously ill. Over several years, she sold a good part of the property to pay for treatment, but finally she died in 1991. The five orphans are now alone and without resources. They are the real victims of this custom.

All human beings are sick, the first sickness of all being sin, the state of disobedience and revolt against the creator. Added to this are physical, mental and other ills. We all need treatment. Healing from sin lies in the return to obedience to the ever-forgiving God. For other ills, the creator has provided all we need, in particular the healing plants (cf. Ezek. 47:12 and Rev. 22:2).

Our ancestors knew the qualities of the plants and were skilled in using them. The missionaries committed a serious error in dismissing this knowledge as satanic, so that thousands of people skilled in the medicinal use of these plants died without passing their knowledge on. It is quite true that in Africa "with every old person who dies, it is a library that burns".

Christians must make it their mission to use the little knowledge that still remains to good purpose. The prayers accompanying the use of these traditional medicines make this an effective instrument of healing whose value has been proved on many occasions.

While our faith in the creator of all things calls us to use these remedies which God has made freely available to us, Africa's current social and economic crisis obliges us to do so. Promoting research into traditional medicines is a challenge that should be picked up by the church as an institution, and feminist theologians can encourage their community to do this at a time when many people rush anxiously to the chemist's shop, only to re-emerge downcast because they cannot afford the increasingly expensive medicines.

The church is there to bear witness to its hope at all times, especially in periods of extreme difficulty. Jesus cared for human beings in their wholeness — spirit, body and soul. He healed them by his word and also by elements taken from nature. As our lives must follow the model given us by Jesus Christ, the practice of healing by plants or other natural elements is an example to us.

Struggling for social justice

Spiritual, economic and social well-being appears in the New Testament as a sign of the kingdom of God and of salvation (cf. Luke 4:18-21). Jesus' miracles were intended to liberate human beings from all the forms of alienation and injustice which prevented them from living life to the full. Yet nearly two thousand years after Jesus Christ, social injustice still reigns supreme in the world, and Africa experiences the reality of it every day. The great powers have reduced the other countries to the status of economic slaves and beggars. In Benin, 40 percent of the population lives below the poverty line, while in Zaire the figure may be as high as 80 percent.

Most countries in Africa south of the Sahara are in a difficult economic and political situation. Africa is sick; it is suffering from general and widespread impoverishment. It is the victim not only of the industrialized countries, but also of some of its own children, including political leaders who are so spiritually and morally bankrupt that they feel no shame at living on an island of opulence in the midst of an ocean of sordid poverty and death.

According to Susan George in *A Fate Worse Than Death*, there are 2500 immensely rich families in Zaire and 27 million people living in total destitution. Zaire's foreign debt amounts to US$5000 million, a sum that corresponds to the amount misappropriated by General Mobutu and his family.

In every situation of crisis and oppression women are doubly oppressed. They are often exposed to violence — rape, prostitution, murder. They become objects at the mercy of soldiers and other lawless men.

In this almost apocalyptic setting (think of what has happened in Rwanda during 1994), how do the church and its feminist theologians bear witness to the hope that is in them? What can they do to contribute to the reign of justice and peace? Those churches which have been accustomed to the policy of the outstretched hand towards the "mother" or "older sister" churches of the West must look with new eyes on their own congregations which are brimming over with human resources and potential.

The challenge is how better to organize and motivate the vital strength represented by young people and women. Young people must be prepared to take on adult responsibilities in all aspects of social life. Women represent an inexhaustible source of initiative with an extraordinary productive output; and as the bearers of life they will not allow life to be lost without fighting to the bitter end. But they are hard-pressed by the effects of the crisis, and it will be for the church to support them in their struggle.

What might women theologians do so that the Lord's promise of life in its fullness (John 10:10) may become a reality, both spiritually and materially, here and now? We shall speak of dogmatics, of hermeneutics, of course. That is very necessary. But we must equally take an interest in the material living conditions of our sisters in all continents, most of whom are engaged in a constant hand-to-hand battle against poverty.

Acts of faith and concrete commitments are what is needed to make feminist theology more credible; a theology of struggle to raise women up and restore them to the place which God gave them in the community.

* * *

The ever-growing number of problems facing the human community and the church tends to make life a burden rather than a joy. When will we rediscover the peace which God alone gives us? When will we overcome the sin which reigns supreme around us and often within us?

In this unending struggle we have the support of God's mercy and love. The faithful and compassionate God of the Exodus guides the destiny of his creation. God's words to Moses about Israel's oppression in Egypt speak to all who suffer in the world: "I have seen the affliction of my people... and have heard their cry because of their taskmasters; I know their sufferings, and I have come down to deliver them" (Ex. 3:7).

In my region these words of comfort can only lead God's people to pray and to work for the task of reconstruction in Africa. The theological work to be undertaken here is both "theology in the theoretical sense of a rigorous search for intellectual understanding of the faith, and theology in the practical sense of work for concrete changes in life and in society, starting with church communities as a motor force for far-reaching change and a real source of strength in the reconstruction of the African continent".[2]

There are two aspects to this reconstruction. One aspect is general; the other involves re-examining the place and role of women in order to do justice to them, to give them their rightful place as valued citizens fighting for a more human and united church and society. If we are to survive we must unite and bar the way to all forms of discrimination. The church's special mission is to work for the unity of humankind, starting from the Christian community, recalling Jesus' prayer "that they may become completely one, so that the world may know that you have sent me and have loved them even as you have loved me" (John 17:23). Such is the Lord's will for the well-being of humanity and the realization of God's reign on earth.

NOTES

[1] Jean-Marie Aubert, *L'exil féminin*, Paris, Cerf, 1988, p. 247.
[2] Ka-Mara, *Foi chrétienne, crise africaine et reconstruction de l'Afrique*, Lomé, Clé, 1991.

Cultural Hermeneutics:
An African Contribution

MUSIMBI KANYORO

Certain recent situations have prompted me to think about culture. Often culture is something subconscious, so ingrained in us that we do not hear or see ourselves within our cultural skin. The objective of this paper is to encourage some more analytical thinking about culture by introducing a few stations on my own journey of thought.

I was very involved with non-governmental organizations (NGOs) in connection with the World Conference on Human Rights (Vienna 1993). A strong argument was put forward, mainly by Asian and African governments, that human rights are culturally determined and therefore we cannot speak about a universal understanding of human rights. China took the lead in this debate, with support from many other states. Critics of this argument quickly pointed to the human rights record of the nations that were making it. We accused them of wanting to hide something, and it is evident that nations like China — and my own country Kenya — are vulnerable to this charge.

The women at the Vienna conference worked very hard to put women's human rights on the agenda, and we succeeded. At the daily women's caucuses, we struggled to maintain a united front on the universality issue because we saw so many possibilities of using culture to explain away the violation of women's rights. We were greatly helped by the current worldwide awareness of how violence against women defies all borders of culture, race, geography and class. Media coverage of the horrendous use of rape in the former Yugoslavia was also a fresh memory.

Yet beneath this united front was a discomfort raised only in faint voices. The common agenda of getting women to the discussion table of the UN member states was our immediate priority; and although some of us saw possibilities in the culture argument, we did not at that time want to deal with the difficult double-edged nature of culture. I remember an informal conversation while walking to lunch with a woman from Pakistan. We found ourselves talking about all the women who have been and are being raped in situations of war around the world. If Bosnia were not in Europe, we wondered, would there have been such extensive press coverage? And if there were, would global solidarity have been mobilized to the same extent?

The question arises for me again as I see the international coverage of Rwanda and other places in conflict. Could we have done it in any other way in Vienna? Or were we being dishonest with one another and to each other as women when we decided not even to discuss the culture argument in connection with the international determination of human rights? Was this another case in which women stand for a cause only to be forgotten after it is won? Were we standing in solidarity with the global women's agenda, knowing full well that we are only marginally part of that agenda?

I recall a presentation made by Nashilogo Elago, a Namibian woman, in a workshop in Bossey in 1988. She said many black women in Namibia had been raped by white occupying soldiers from South Africa. When the women took the matter to the courts, they were told that it was not a serious issue because, culturally, black people enjoy sex and African women are used to rough treatment in their homes. Later, I met this kind of thinking again when a missionary doctor stopped in Geneva to brief the ecumenical organizations during the terrible early days of the Liberian war. After telling of the horrible killings and looting, he spoke of the widespread rape of women, which no media reports had mentioned. In the discussion that followed, some of us focused on the question of how to help these women. The missionary doctor replied that he saw no possible traumatic effects of rape on them.

Encounters such as these have led me to seek more focus on the issue of culture in all its forms. It seems to me that there has been little mature analysis of or dialogue on culture in ecumenical and international circles. Rather, culture is a euphemism used to explain biases, justify actions that might otherwise be challenged and foster diversity at the expense of unity. There is need to challenge this and to face what it takes to have sincere dialogue on culture. Having underscored the universality of the subordination of women, perhaps women can give credibility to this debate; and the current ecumenical focus on gospel and cultures may be one forum in which Christian women can speak about their experiences.

Let me use an example to illustrate the conditions which might create a possible safe environment for cultural dialogue. In a January 1994 conference in Nairobi of African women theologians, Denise Ackermann described her own theological journey as a white South African who grew up in the system of apartheid. She was challenged to undertake this painful journey by the feminist analysis which supports doing theology from our experience. Yet she felt left out of the theology represented, for example, by the book *The Will to Arise: Women, Tradition and the Church in Africa*,[1] in which African Christian and Muslim women speak of their religious experiences within the setting of African cultures.

These authors search for the female face of God through analysis of their experiences in culture and in religion, especially the rites of passage. They explore the structures and institutions established to support and maintain these rites: rituals, taboos, initiations that accompany birthing, growing up, marriage, mothering, death; ceremonies to celebrate those occasions; practices and precautions to maintain and to ensure a future. They discuss such issues as naming rituals, fertility, dowry, property, ownership, widowhood, sexuality, polygamy. The experiences that weave the theology around these issues are not in the realm of Denise Ackermann's African world, though she is familiar with some of them because she was born in Africa, has daily contact with indigenous Africans and is well read. But did she have a right to be involved in the depth of the analysis that the other African women are doing? How far could she go with her critique? Would her critique inevitably be from the safely distant vantage point from which she has been socialized to regard traditions of indigenous African people? Would we accept it or would that kind of participation in our experiences estrange us from each other and create division?

The Cape Town Circle of Concerned African Women in Theology, a group made up of blacks, Asians, coloured and whites whose religious experiences are Muslim, Christian and African indigenous, discussed these concerns. Their dialogue led them to conclude that cultural critique is possible only where the vulnerability of all the participants is transparent. Denise was challenged to lay herself bare on the issue of the culture of apartheid.

Listening to her paper in Nairobi made me think more seriously of the theology that African women are doing. Upon reflection I concluded that theology whose method is informed by cultural analysis is not peculiar to Africa, although it is more prevalent there. It is what Asian women are doing when they address issues like dowry and the burning of brides in

India, what black Brazilians are doing as they ask for a recognition of their indigenous spirituality, what womanist theologians do when they take into account the peculiar cultural distinctions of African-American women.

It seems to me that something significant is happening here to theological analysis. This new aspect of analysis, brought to theology mainly by studies of women of the south, deserves its rightful place among theological paradigms. It could be called cultural hermeneutics. Cultural hermeneutics has the potential to enable us to develop a vision for mature cultural dialogues. The complexities inherent in cultural debate require a space and safe environment of mutual trust and mutual vulnerability in order for dialogue to take place.

Applying cultural hermeneutics to the biblical text

Recognition of the universality of women's subordination and oppression is the basis of all feminist work. But divergences in the direction of the feminist critique of culture and in the priorities of the struggle on issues of culture have divided and silenced women. Cultural hermeneutics can open our eyes to possibilities which might move us to different commitments. Let me illustrate using both the Bible and the experiences of African women. By so doing, I hope to show what I believe to be some difficult questions confronting African women reading the Bible and to demonstrate that African women are asking something new from the theological debate in general and from women's theology in particular.

The biblical story is that of the three women Naomi, Ruth and Orpah, as it is found in the Old Testament book of Ruth. These three widows must begin a new life after the deaths of their husbands. Orpah chooses to return to her own people, and the Bible is silent about what happened to her; in fact, she is mentioned only to contrast her with Ruth, who chose to remain faithful to Naomi and Naomi's people. Alice L. Laffy has done a very thorough feminist analysis of this passage and also presents a summary of other feminist views.[2] Some emphasize God's empowering of the powerless through Ruth's marriage to Boaz and the subsequent birth of a son. Others point to the friendship of two women of different ages and different nationalities. Still others highlight the courage of the women as they make decisions for their new lives.

Critics denounce the culture which made women feel powerless if they were not attached to a man, the custom of a widow marrying the next of kin and the lack of choice and opportunity for women. But this is as far as the critique goes — as if this is a story from long ago and these issues are no longer relevant today.

In fact, the practice of requiring widows to marry the brother of their dead husband persists in many parts of Africa, and the church and women themselves have sometimes seen this text as endorsing this cultural practice. Our experiences in these circumstances demand that we stay longer with the text and find a way to rescue the characters from cultural bondage. Women who choose to be Orpahs have no models of blessing from the Bible. How do we support Orpahs? What blessings could we imagine for Orpah, especially when compared with the blessings that befell Ruth when she succumbed to certain cultural possibilities — a reward which culminates in her taking a place in the lineage of salvation (Matt. 1:5)?

Our concern with the biblical text is not just to condemn the culture but to seek tools to analyze culture in order to reach out to women who are in bondage to it. So we continue the exegesis of Ruth by enquiring of women what message this story conveys to them. Does it encourage them to succumb to cultural expectations? What is the message for women who want to be different? How do we imagine the life of Orpah? What blessings and problems accompanied her? Why? Could we be Orpahs? How does an Orpah mobilize collective solidarity? How does she face communal criticism? The questions are endless. We also ask many questions to Ruth and Naomi.

The feminist analysis of patriarchy sometimes approaches women's oppression by pointing to the men as the oppressors. This approach is a non-starter in Africa. While African women acknowledge the oppression of men, they do not use the direct method of throwing stones, reasoning that this would pose a major threat to women's solidarity. It is easy to discredit struggles that centre on cultural oppression with the excuse that they break up the community. Moreover, when dealing with cultural matters, there is a need for collective solidarity. Cultural oppression cannot be addressed in singularity. Since the custodians of indigenous cultures often have little contact with other cultures, a valid analysis must include their views.

For us as African feminists this is crucial if our feminism is not to be seen merely as a bourgeois deviation resulting from the cultural imperialism of Western women. Lack of consensus on what, when and how to be critical of cultures makes it difficult for African women to mount a collective resistance either to alien cultural values or to oppressive elements of indigenous cultures. It is difficult when solidarity among women cannot be obtained. This lack of collective solidarity is not a matter of a generation gap or different levels of education or varying religious affiliation, but of cultural loyalty. Rituals and initiation practices are one area in which it is very difficult for women to reach a consensus. This is not a sign of lack of courage or inability to confront issues, but of counting the cost and taking stock of the gains and losses. Cultural ideologies regarding gender roles and power in society are deeply embedded in our lived experience. Even on issues of violence and how male power over women is maintained, it is no easier for African women to agree jointly to condemn the men. In addition to the threat to solidarity among women, some African women reason that they want a future in which men are friends. Building that future does not begin by attacking men but by finding methods of bringing change together with them. This is of course a tall order, but it is the reality of the lived experience of African women.

Another point that needs to be confronted is that the practice of institutionalized cultural violence has ensured that women are not only victims but also, more often than not, perpetrators. Who enforce inhuman rituals on widows in Africa and Asia? Who are the excisors of the female? Who are the instigators of divorce or polygamy in the case of wives unable to give birth to children or specifically to male children? These are areas of *women's* violence against women. We have to break the vicious circle of women violating other women in the name of culture. We cannot continue to bemoan the socialization we have had when lives are at stake. That is what some of our African governments do when they blame every tragedy on colonialism and refuse to be accountable for their own part in the calamity of our continent. Women must come of age, confront ourselves and also address women as the cause of oppression. This is not a refusal to address male oppression, but rather a way of empowering women to remove the log in our own eyes so that we can see clearly the log in other people's eyes.

When I read the story of Sarah and Hagar through the eyes of Elsa Tamez, I was delighted to discover that God had a place for Hagar.[3] But Sarah and Hagar are not biblical women for me. They are my family. I have lived in the middle of their struggle all my life. I am part of their fights day in and day out. I am not able to see one as the oppressor and exonerate the other. I see envy, jealousy, revenge, competition and many more ugly things. As an adult Bible-reading woman, I am not looking for models of behaviour but rather for clues as to what might change behaviour. I don't want to see the help which comes to one of them and begin the vicious circle of envy. I want to see them together, refusing the system that promotes their behaviour. I don't want to sustain the syndrome of blaming the other and not taking personal responsibility. This is where the difficulties in reading the Bible lie for those of us who come from cultures which closely mirror the practices of biblical times.

Let us look at another example. Women and work is an issue that feminist theory has addressed in great detail. Many women have found liberation in moving from the household into paid work. Their personal freedom of movement and earnings have been enhanced. But what has this done to those who stayed at home and to the work they do? Sometimes even a "women's reading" of the Bible does not answer the questions that bother us. Take the Martha and Mary story (Luke 10:38-42; John 11:1-44). In that story we have found liberation in the affirmation by Jesus of Mary's desire for knowledge. That is good. But what about Martha? A majority of women in Africa are Marthas. We live on a continent stricken with all sorts of calamities. Hospitality and service are the true hope for the millions of starving and dying. We are a continent where more than 60 percent of women are illiterate, and no change in this seems in view. This means that for us celebrating Mary's privileged position of learning is very painful. We do it, with reservations, as we see that the privileges of material wealth and Western knowledge determine who lives and who dies. We as African women doing theology are among the privileged, but we carry a burden. How shall we do theology that gives hope to our continent? In *Household of Freedom*, Letty Russell has argued that no theology is adequate if it cannot speak to and from the experiences of its participants, its doers and its hearers. "Women's experiences include the biological and cultural experiences of being female as well as the feminist experience, the political experience of those who advocate a change of society to include both women and men as human beings."[4] We are a long way from this.

Questions for feminist theories

Here are two testimonies by university-educated women in Mali, interviewed by Awa Thiam:[5]

Case 1 (35 years old, working in a government department):

I had just turned 12 when I was excised... The excisor was an old woman belonging to the blacksmiths' caste. Here in Mali, it is usually women of this caste who practice ablation of the clitoris and infibulation.

On the threshold of the hut, my aunts exchanged the customary greetings and left me in the hands of the excisor... Once I was inside, the women began to sing my praises, to which I turned a deaf ear, as I was overcome with terror... "Lie down," the excisor suddenly said to me... Two women on each side of me pinned to the ground... First I underwent the ablation of the labia minora, and then of the clitoris... It was a rule that the girls of my age did not weep in this situation. I broke a rule... I was bleeding. The blood flowed in torrents. Then they applied a mixture of butter and medicinal herbs which stopped the bleeding. Never had I felt such excruciating pain. After this, the women let go their grasp, freeing my mutilated body... "You can stand up now"... Then they forced me, not only to walk back to join the other girls who had already been excised, but to dance with them... It was months before I was completely well... Everyone mocked me as I hadn't been brave, they said.

Case 2 (26 years old, divorced with one child):

I was excised as a child... I am talking about my personal experience. Today I am happy I had the excision operation... It has fulfilled its function as far as I am concerned. I've been divorced for four years and I've never for one moment felt the desire to run after a man, or felt the absence of sexual relations to be a vital lack. That indicates to some extent the function of excision... It allows a woman to be in control of her own body. And that is why I don't in any way consider it as a mutilation... I can't think of excision as practised by our elders as being a mutilation. In fact it boils down to what the intention is, and with them, it isn't to mutilate.

Today through media campaigns backed by medical reports and novels such as Alice Walker's *Possessing the Secret of Joy*, it has been proved that female circumcision is harmful to the health of women. Feminists see it as a destruction of women's sexual pleasure in the interest of male sexuality. Yet millions of women who continue to practise it see it as their cultural heritage and as affirming their dignity within society. In fact for some, as the second case above illustrates, it is the path to freedom over their own bodies. Feminists have advocated the right of women to freedom over their bodies and their sexuality. The accepted methods include choices in marriage and sexual orientation, control over reproductivity and of course the freedom to make decisions. But feminists often assume that there are specific right ways to do these things. What about women who choose other ways, including their cultural ways, to reach the same goal?

Here is a real challenge to the current collective struggle to outlaw certain traditional practices, calling for the formulation of an alternative to the feminist analysis which speaks to the experiences not only of women who are against traditional practices, but also of those who find personal empowerment in the practices.

It might be argued that empowering has to be a liberating experience that gives a full humanity to women (Rosemary Ruether). But who judges what is liberating — the woman herself or someone else? Can we accept that female circumcision has liberated the woman in case 2? What cultures determine the choices that are good for individual women? If women have to change a culture, what process should be used towards that change? What support systems will be made available to fill the void? Unless a theoretical analysis sees the people involved, its claim for universal validity will not stand.

Establishing women's explanations for culture

Much work is needed on the history of culture and the structures that maintain it. We need to establish how women explain their cultural practices and then discover the source of such explanations. Sometimes there are surprises. For example, Awa Thiam reports that there is a well-known myth among Muslim and Christian West Africans that female circumcision is good for women because it was started by women. At the command of God Sarah circumcised Hagar. The myth goes like this:

Long before the time of Mahout, there was a prophet named Ibrahima (Abraham), who was married to his cousin Sarata (Sara). He went up to the land of Gerar, where reigned king Abimelech, who delighted in taking to himself all men's wives who were remarkable for their beauty. Now it happened that Sarata was unusually fair. And the king did not hesitate to try to take her from her husband. A supernatural power prevented him from taking advantage of her, which so astonished him that he set her free. And he restored her back to her husband and made her the gift of a handmaid named Hadiara (Hagar).

Sarata and her husband lived together for a long time but Sarata bore Ibrahima no child. And eventually, Ibrahima took Hadiara to wife; some said that it was Sarata who said to her husband that he should take her handmaid to wife since she herself could bear no children. And so Sarata and Hadiara became co-wives to Ibrahima and Hadiara bore him a son and his name was Ismaila (Ishmael) and Sarata also bore a son to Ibrahima and he was called Ishaga (Isaac). In the course of time, the relationship between the two women deteriorated. And so it came to pass that one day Sarata excised Hadiara. Some say that she only pierced her ears while others maintain she did indeed excise her.[6]

Neither the Bible nor the Quran makes any mention of excision. But how did this myth get to the women of Africa? Why does it circulate only among the groups that circumcise women? Culture has been a dominant feature in African theology. Christian missionaries tended to see African cultures as totally barbaric. Liberal explorers romanticized them, in the belief that the African would outgrow them with the adoption of the new "civilization".

In the 1960s and 1970s, African theologians (mainly male) began to do a theology of inculturation in reaction to the Western cultural imperialism that came with Christianity and colonialism. The general conviction behind this is that the message of Christ can be dynamic and communicative to all people in all cultures, at all times. For Africa, inculturation is a form of liberation theology. It decries the Western imperialism in which Christianity was wrapped and exported to Africa.

Simon Maimela describes "inculturation" as "an approach which is characterized by the attempt to marry Christianity with the African world view, so that Christianity could speak [to Africans] with the African idiom and accent". Hence African inculturation theology has to do with the Africanizing of Christianity.[7] African women theologians have argued that the cry to regain our culture is artificial, because we never lost it in the first place. The parts of culture that were touched were rather artificial and what actually happened was the addition of foreign cultural elements to African cultures. Women have given evidence for these arguments, but there is still reluctance on the part of men genuinely to come to terms with the question of women and culture.

Descriptions of aspects of African culture exist in many publications. Historically, such written works are remnants of diaries, memoirs, ethnographic monographs and anthropological treatises. The authors were merchants, missionaries, colonialists, anthropologists and, later, African men. Accordingly, their research on women was not only brief but also second-hand and often distorted. Most of these writers, women included, were socialized within pietistic, patriarchal or Victorian value systems. Under these circumstances, the task of African women is not only to correct past records but also to provide fresh data on the variety of women's experiences and the nature of their struggles against oppression. The objective is not merely to write women back into history, but also to record gender struggles as defined by history, culture, race and class structures in Africa. Some aspects being encountered share the analysis done by women from other parts of our global community, but in the area of culture we see that our experiences offer a certain uniqueness that is specific to Africa.

NOTES

[1] Eds Mercy Amba Oduyoye and Musimbi R.A. Kanyoro, Maryknoll, NY, Orbis, 1992.

[2] Alice L. Laffy, *An Introduction to the Old Testament: A Feminist Perspective*, Philadelphia, Fortress, 1988, pp.205-10.

[3] See Elsa Tamez, "The Woman Who Complicated the History of Salvation", in *New Eyes for Reading: Biblical and Theological Reflections by Women from the Third World*, eds John S. Pobee and Bärbel von Wartenberg-Potter, Geneva, WCC, 1986.

[4] Letty Russell, *Household of Freedom*, Philadelphia, Westminster, 1987.

[5] Awa Thiam, *Black Sisters Speak Out: Feminism and Oppression in Black Africa*, London, Pluto Press, 1986, pp.63ff.

[6] *Ibid.*, p.59.

[7] Simon Maimela, in *EATWOT Africa Conference Report 1991;* cf. M.J. Waliggo, ed., *Inculturation: Its Meaning and Urgency*, Nairobi, St Paul Publications, 1986, p.12.

Feminist Theology in Asia:
An Overview

MARY-JOHN MANANZAN, OSB

The context of feminist theologizing in Asia is the situation and struggle of its people, especially of its women. Asia is a vast continent, rich in human and natural resources yet suffering from widespread poverty. Most Asian countries have a long history of colonialism and almost all are prey to imperialism. Although all have gained political independence, what was done by colonizers is now perpetrated by local elites, who connive with foreign powers to exploit the great majority of the people. Asian nations are dependent on foreign investments and groan under the weight of increasing indebtedness. Free-trade zones exploit Asia's cheap labour, while unemployment and rising prices have sent many Asians to look for work in other parts of the world. The distribution of wealth is unequal, and the stratification of society into classes and castes has led to violence in various countries. Militarization is prevalent, and in many countries defence expenditures eat up a large percentage of the national budget.

In this situation Asian women suffer double and triple oppression. Aside from discrimination and subordination, women experience various forms of domestic and social violence. They are also victims of trafficking in different forms: as prostitutes, mail-order brides, overseas contract workers, domestic helpers and entertainers.

But there is also a growing political and social consciousness in Asia. People's organizations, women's organizations, ecological, peace and justice movements are raising people's awareness and mobilizing them to struggle for their rights and for a more humane society. Among the most militant of these social movements is the women's movement, which is the immediate context of feminist theologizing.

The EATWOT commission on women

In the 1970s a few consultations of Asian church women were convoked and associations of theologically trained women were formed in several countries. However, these were concerned with the participants' courses of study, status, working conditions and role in the church rather than in actually theologizing from the point of view of Asian women. Systematic efforts towards feminist theologizing came in the 1980s, with the establishment of the women's commission of the Ecumenical Association of Third World Theologians (EATWOT).

Already in EATWOT's 1981 general assembly in New Delhi, what Mercy Oduyoye would call an "irruption within an irruption" took place: the realization among EATWOT women that although their male counterparts were progressive theologians, they were gender-blind. No women were present as resource persons, and the women felt that their theological contributions were not taken seriously enough by their male colleagues. According to Virginia Fabella,

> to EATWOT women, "the irruption within the irruption"... signified both a protest and a demand. Without many words, the women made it known that they no longer wanted to be token presences or fill quotas at EATWOT meetings, or just be politely listened to and then ignored. EATWOT structures and practices would henceforth have to reflect the unity and equality in Christ that Christians claim. EATWOT agendas would need to address sexism-in-community as a theological issue if indeed the association seeks a truly just world.[1]

Two years later EATWOT women took concrete steps to realize their dream. At an EATWOT-sponsored dialogue in Geneva between first- and third-world theologians, feminist theology proved to be "the most fully developed theology of liberation in the first world and created the greatest impact on the gathering.[2] Sexism became one of the major issues in the conference; and this had a direct impact on the decision to establish an EATWOT women's commission, both to meet the need of third-world women theologians to set priorities and an agenda and to provide a concrete and immediate response to the intense discussion of women's oppression by the conference.

The tasks of the women's commission were: (1) to make a structural analysis of the situation of women: economic, political, socio-cultural and religious; (2) to discuss the patriarchal element in theology today; (3) to reformulate theology from the perspective of full humanity.

Several themes for developing a feminist liberation theology from the perspective of third-world women were suggested:
1) the oppression of women and women's responses in society and church;
2) social analysis of each country's economic structure, political system and social, cultural and religious situation;
3) theological reflection: hermeneutical analysis of the Bible; study of myths, folklore, legends, indigenous religions; reflection on God-talk and woman, Christology and woman, Mariology, pneumatology and woman, ecclesiology and woman;
4) emerging forms of spirituality.

Following a series of national consultations bringing together women theologians in various countries of Asia, an Asian continental consultation took place in Manila in November 1985, with the theme "Total Liberation from Asian Women's Perspective". Twenty-seven women from seven Asian countries attended the consultation, which included exposures to urban and rural areas in the Philippines, reports of the national consultations, biblical reflections, creative liturgical celebration and theological reflections on women's oppression as a sinful situation, God-talk and women, women and the Christ event, women and the faith community, women and Mary and women and the Holy Spirit.

This consultation introduced Asian women into the working methodology of feminist theology. This meant contextualizing the reflection of women in the different countries in their concrete situations. It also meant collective initiation into the unaccustomed effort of writing composite papers. It called for the creation of original methods of expression, such as mural painting to convey women's theological insights artistically. Cushions and mattresses on the floor made it possible for the women to discuss in a relaxed position, creating an atmosphere conducive to free-flowing and in-depth sharing.

Among the theological conclusions enumerated in the final statement of the consultation were:
1) Oppression of women is sinful. This systemic sin is rooted in organized structures — economic, political and cultural — with patriarchy as an overarching reality that oppresses women.
2) The patriarchal churches have contributed to the subjugation and marginalization of women.
3) Theology itself, in its premises, traditions and beliefs, has blurred the image of God that women are.

4) The bias against women in Christian tradition buttresses male-oriented Asian religious beliefs.

At the same time the participants rediscovered empowering elements in their Christian faith: Jesus' saving mission, which includes all, his supportive attitude towards women, the creative power of the Holy Spirit to overcome the forces of sin and death, the Mary of the Magnificat as an inspiration to struggle for justice and greater humanity for the poor and oppressed. There was a renewed commitment to this struggle, especially for confronting patriarchal structures. The consultation called for a solidarity beyond gender and race towards a new community of men and women characterized by justice, equality, peace and love.

New insights in methodology and hermeneutics

On the basis of the experiences in the national and regional consultations, the following elements of methodology in Asian feminist theologizing may be identified:

1. *Contextualization:* The starting point of theologizing is the experience of Asian women and their struggle in a male-dominated world. In the act of telling their stories, consciously and politically, women begin to understand themselves and their reality better.

2. *New biblical hermeneutics:* A new reading of the Bible must emerge which reinterprets passages that confirm subordination of and discrimination against women in the light of their cultural context.

3. *Religious and cultural critique:* The plurality of cultures and religions in Asia calls for a critical study to identify both liberating and oppressive forces in all of them.

4. *Recovery of the authentic value of women's experience:* Women recognize their religious heritage, but they reject imposed tradition and realize that their spiritual heritage goes beyond institutionalized religion and official theology.

5. *Reinterpretation and reformulation:* As women bring their own experiences and the analysis of their situations into the religious traditions, new translations, new interpretations and new language emerge. Religious insights are expressed in a variety of forms and symbols.

6. *New visions:* Women envision and struggle to realize new possibilities for community and social relationships. Asian feminist theology is not mere academic theology. It leads to liberating action. The condition for Asian feminist theologizing is involvement in the women's struggle. It is through political action for social transformation that women's theologizing is verified.

Nine Asian women attended the intercontinental encounter of EATWOT women in Oaxtepec, Mexico, in December 1986, whose theme was "Doing Theology from the Third World Women's Perspective", and whose main task was to identify commonalities and differences in doing theology in the various regions. Several important insights emerged:

1. The oppression of women is an abiding reality in all spheres of life: economic, political, social, cultural, sexual and religious. But women in all continents have organized themselves to struggle for their rights. Among these efforts, theologizing is a specific move by which women struggle for their right to life.

2. Third-world women's spirituality, rooted in action for justice, is intertwined with theologizing. This spirituality is passionate and compassionate.

3. The Bible plays a vital role in the lives of women and in their struggle for liberation. Instead of rejecting the Bible because of its patriarchal element, the participants felt the need of delving deeper into it, rejecting the patriarchal crust and highlighting the neglected elements which portray women as God's co-workers and agents of life.

4. By and large women are still excluded from the leadership of the churches in the different continents. The participants called for new ways of being church which reflect more truly God's reign and the new creation.

5. Christology is central in third-world women's theology, but it must be contextualized in the oppressive and painful realities of each continent, relating both to the causes of people's suffering and misery and the efforts of people for justice.

6. Without losing its scientific seriousness, theology done by third-world women is grounded in experience, in affection, in *life*. In other words, it is not only a theology of the mind but also of the womb. Like spirituality, it is passionate and compassionate.

An Asian women's consultation to formulate an Asian feminist hermeneutics was done in two phases: the first in Seoul, the second in Madras. The consensus after the second meeting was that Asian women's hermeneutical principle should affirm:

1) the full humanity of women in an authentic and inclusive community of peace, joy and freedom, based on just relationships;
2) the integrity of creation;
3) the feminine creative principle as life-giving and life-enhancing;

4) the prophetic and alternative voice and action of women in liberation movements;
5) the solidarity of women among themselves and with others supporting each one's struggle as well as the people's movements.

Women and violence

The EATWOT general assembly in Nairobi in 1992 restored the international coordination of the women's commission. Since Oaxtepec the women's commissions on each continent had worked without much communication with the others. International and continental coordinators were elected and a theme was chosen for the next five years: "Spirituality for Life: Women Struggling against Violence".

The Nairobi conference was also significant for the marked change evident in the relationship between the men and women theologians. Unlike New Delhi in 1981, the women felt that they were taken seriously. In an Asian worship service, the women invited the men to place their symbols of solidarity with the women's struggle in the middle of the assembly and they did so. At the closing liturgy, the men made another symbolic gesture by kneeling down to ask pardon from the women for their silence or participation in the oppression of women. An African woman gave them absolution, expressing the hope that this touching gesture be concretized in action.

Between 1992 and 1994, women EATWOT members in various countries of Asia convened national consultations on the theme agreed upon in Nairobi; and in January 1994, 18 delegates from these countries met in Manila for a regional consultation.

Delegates narrated poignant stories of violence against women in their various national situations. In addition, an exposure visit in Manila gave them some common experience of such cases and of efforts by women to alleviate the suffering that results. Commonalities and uniqueness in the reports were identified and analyzed.

To add to the data, there were inputs about violence against women in the context of Buddhism, Hinduism, Confucianism and primal religion. Then the delegates reflected on several aspects of theology that relate to violence against women: (1) the image of God and Christology; (2) marriage and sexuality; (3) ecclesiology and ministry; (4) mission; (5) moral theology and spirituality. The main insights were:

1. The most harmful image of God is the personification of God as a male, a warrior, the Absolute Other up in heaven, the jealous father who demands the sacrifice of his only son in atonement for sins. This has been

used to legitimize child abuse and to foster a "victim attitude" among women. The image of Jesus as sacrificial lamb has likewise induced women to follow the path of "innocent victimhood". There is a need to reconstruct the life-giving images which are fluid and dynamic, compassionate and liberating, cosmic and encompassing of all creation, space and time.

2. The mental conditioning of women with regard to their sexuality is already a form of violence against them. There is a hierarchical mode in marriage and family life which is oppressive to wives and children; the husband's sense of proprietorship sets up women to be victims of male whim and aggression. What is needed is an holistic view of human sexuality which encompasses one's total self-expression and is based on mutuality. There is furthermore a need to develop a healthy theology of body and to demystify the cult of virginity.

3. The institutional church is not only patriarchal, hierarchical and clerical but also colonialistic, capitalistic, feudal and fundamentalist at its core. It produces a ministry that is dualistic, power-oriented, ritual-centred and discriminatory against women. There is a need for a new *ecclesia* that is an *oikos* of God, an inclusive community that encompasses all beings.

4. The hierarchical view of the world taught in a predominantly Western mission theology has reinforced the lower status of women. There is a call for an alternative theology of mission whose main thrust is the search for fullness of life, *purnam*. For women this means the elimination of all forms of violence, drawing strength from Christianity as well as from other religions.

5. The morality that has evolved in patriarchal society has crippled women's minds and produced guilt complexes that have infringed on their freedom. So pervasive has this been — in the home, in education and indeed in all areas of life — that it has become a structural sin. There is a need to develop a cosmic spirituality by returning to our life-giving roots and actively participating in creating a society based on just, right and harmonious relationships. Cosmic spirituality includes promoting not only human but also ecological wholeness.

Concrete forms of action were agreed upon, including development of a theology of sexuality, introduction of feminist studies in seminaries and schools and working with local groups in churches. Research projects were assigned on the spirituality of primal religions, the image of God and Christology as relating to violence against women, deeper studies of religious traditions and cultures of Asia, case studies of violence against women as well as successful strategies used. Of these plans the final statement says:

> We see these tasks as our collective responsibilities as Asian EATWOT women. We realize the immensity of what we have set for ourselves. But the reality of violence against women in Asia urgently calls for action. Recalling the stories we shared in the beginning we are determined to change the patriarchal scripts written of Asian women's lives. We want to turn those stories of woes into stories of survival and success. Thus no task is too hard nor too great if it means new life for women and new women's stories to be told.

NOTES

[1] Virginia Fabella, *Beyond Bonding: A Third World Woman's Theological Journey*, Manila, EATWOT and Institute of Women's Studies, 1993, p.31.
[2] *Ibid.*, p.34.

A Short History
of Asian Feminist Theology

SUN AI LEE-PARK

The history of Asian feminist theology is not long. Even in the USA, considered by many as the place where feminist theology had its genesis, it arose only in the 1960s in the wake of the second wave of the women's movement. In the third world feminist theology did not begin to take shape until the 1970s.

This paper will consist of two parts. The first, based on my personal experiences, will make some comments about two organizations important in the development of feminist theology in Asia; the second will mention a few of the individuals making significant contributions to the development of feminist theology in three countries of Asia.

Feminist theologians often refer to women's "lived experiences". The reason for this is that traditional theology has been primarily androcentric, based on men's lived experiences and totally excluding those of women. To be sure, women's lived experiences are varied, and there are as many experiences as there are women in this world. Yet even in this pluralistic situation, we feel that we should be able to find some commonalities in their being women, with all the joys and all the pain and agony of being discriminated against which that brings.

We might divide the commonalities into a number of categories, for example, geographical and historical commonality. We may also find some critical differences, for example, between the middle-class white women who spearheaded the women's movement and black women like Sojourner Truth who came through the experiences of slavery:

> The man over there says women need to be helped into carriages and lifted over ditches, and to have the best place everywhere. Nobody ever helps me into carriages or over puddles, or gives me the best place — and ain't I a woman? [She raised her black arm and said:] Look at my arm! I have ploughed and planted and gathered into barns, and no man could head me —

and ain't I a woman? I could work as much and eat as much as a man — when I could get it — and bear the lash as well! And ain't I a woman? I have borne 13 children, and seen most of 'em sold into slavery, and when I cried out with my mother's grief, none but Jesus heard me — and ain't I a women?[1]

Third world feminist theologians would be very much inclined to identify with these black women, due to our common experiences under colonialism. For example, towards the end of the Pacific war, the Japanese colonial authorities forcibly recruited young Korean women to become sex slaves for Japanese military personnel. The stories of these "comfort women" are heartbreaking. They were victims of double exploitation, as women and as colonized Koreans. The situation of contemporary third world women is similarly characterized by sexist discrimination and neo-colonialist exploitation.

EATWOT and AWRC

One of the things discussed at the meeting of the Ecumenical Association of Third World Theologians (EATWOT) in New Delhi in August 1981 was the plan for an encounter in Geneva the following year between third world theologians and progressive first world theologians, including a large number of feminist theologians. During the Geneva meeting I was asked to be the coordinator of the newly created Asian Women's Commission of EATWOT. Behind the decision to create this and other regional women's commissions lay a history of recurring discrimination against women in EATWOT.

Virginia Fabella, who was the sole woman staff of EATWOT from even before its inception in 1976, recalls that only one woman attended its inaugural meeting in Dar es Salaam, Tanzania — Beatriz Couch from Latin America — and "while the final statement admitted that 'women have been discriminated against and oppressed on all levels of both society and the church', in none of the post-conference assessment was there an allusion to Couch's token presence at Dar".[2]

Again, at EATWOT's third inter-continental dialogue, held in Sri Lanka, "for the first time in an EATWOT statement, the domination and multiple oppression of Asian women was seen as a theological issue to be dealt with, but there was little discussion of it in the actual conference".[3]

During the Geneva meeting, a well-known Western liberation theologian admonished Western feminist theologians of the negative consequences of their influence over third world women theologians, whose priority concern, he said, should be involvement together with male theologians in the liberation struggle. Western feminist theologians should refrain from co-opting third world women into a cause which was ostensibly for the benefit of white women. When this argument more or less silenced the notables among the Western feminist theologians, I intervened quickly to point out its sexist orientation and its sinister and not so subtle intention to divide first world and third world women. It was, I argued, the business of the third world women to decide their own priorities. Within that framework we would build solidarity with our men and with Western feminists, from a third world perspective.

At the Geneva conference, says Virginia Fabella:

> Feminist theology manifested itself as the most fully developed theology of liberation in the first world and created the greatest impact on the gathering. Though they did not speak with one voice, the feminist theologians from Europe and the United States formed an impressive and well-prepared group.[4]

Western women theologians also expressed a desire for a dialogue session with third world women.

To collect third world women theologians' voices, a proposal was presented to the EATWOT executive committee and approved:

> The proposal gave as the main purpose of the Women's Commission to promote a theology of liberation from the perspective of women in the third world, a theology that springs from a critical awareness of women's subjugated position and a commitment to change it. Its specific objectives thus included analyzing women's economic, political, cultural and religious realities within the third world context, as well as discerning the patriarchal elements in theology in order to renew it. The proposal also outlined a progression of work in four phases: from a national level in 1984, to a continental level in 1985, to an intercontinental level in 1986 and finally, to an inter-world or global level in 1987.[5]

Continental coordinators were chosen to organize the consultations in their region and to find suitable contact persons for the national meetings. As Asian coordinator, I wrote many letters regarding EATWOT and raised funds for national meetings. Eight nations participated: India, Sri Lanka, The Philippines, Hong Kong, Korea, Japan, Malaysia and Aotearoa New Zealand. I attended several of the national meetings, and my impression of all these was of creativity and diversity within the overall guidelines.

Our continental conference was held in 1985 in Manila. It was a marvellous meeting, organized by Filipinas and beginning with an exposure trip to get in touch with Philippine realities: a fishing village, plantation workers, urban industrial workers on picket lines and Manila night life. Interpreters enabled us to communicate with these people, and when we returned we shared our experiences. Each nation presented its situation and a biblical reflection on it. During the theological presentations, we were grouped according to themes — Christology, pneumatology, Mariology and spirituality — and a composite paper was prepared from this group work.

The following year the EATWOT general assembly in Oaxtepec, Mexico, was preceded by a third world women's fellowship meeting. This gathering of African, Latin American and Asian women was a first in theological history. Some of the papers from the meeting were later published under the title *With Passion and Compassion* (edited by Virginia Fabella and Mercy Oduyoye). There was also a dialogue session between third world women and black women from the US.

One day, Pura Calo, education secretary of the Christian Conference of Asia, Yvonne Dahlin, women's secretary of the Association of Theological Education in South East Asia (ATESEA), and I had lunch together in Singapore to talk about theological education in Asia. Out of that meeting grew the idea of a conference for Asian women, which was held in Singapore in November 1987 and brought together 34 women from 16 nations. Each participant presented two papers — one on her national situation and biblical reflection on it, the other a theological paper on the chosen theme.

The success of this meeting inspired us to continue, and in September 1988 a core group met in Hong Kong and the Asian Women Resource Centre for Culture and Theology (AWRC) came into being.

In order to offer an impression of the work of EATWOT and AWRC, it may be helpful to look at their treatment of two theological themes: Christology and Mariology.

1. The Christology of EATWOT:

• Even if Christ was male, he was beyond male and female, i.e., he did not use his maleness as a means to dominate and oppress women.

• Focus on Christ as the liberator of all people.[6]

Although a male, Jesus Christ was a great respecter of women. They were his constant companions in ministry, and he gave women a significant role in the proclamation of his message.

People's sufferings are considered as the passion of Christ renewed in the present time. Christ as liberator is seen as the new Christ alive in the people's struggle for freedom and justice and a source of dynamism for it. Moreover, all the religions of Asia have liberative streams, and Asian women are challenged to discover and recover these streams.

2. The Mariology of EATWOT:

Mary is a woman like us, close to us in her refreshing humanity and clearly identified with our world of conflicts in her understanding and solidarity. When Jesus called her "Woman" rather than "Mother" at the wedding feast in Cana and from the cross, he was affirming not only that he values womanhood, but that in the new dispensation being woman has priority over being mother.

How deep must be Mary's compassion for the mothers and wives of political detainees and massacred people who shed blood in denouncing injustices in society. As a mother she instinctively feels for human life... She is truly our sister in faith who committed herself to the coming of the kingdom. She is definitely the closest ally of Asian women in struggling for fuller humanity... We need the example of her strength — we who have to fight male domination, we in third world countries who have to face the present risks and challenges posed by the reign of domination. It gives us courage to overcome our fears and sense of hopelessness.[7]

3. The Christology of AWRC:

The first paragraph of the composite paper from the 1987 Singapore conference summarizes AWRC's Christological ideas:

The Asian women's understanding of Jesus is that he transcends the evil orders of patriarchy. He is the prophetic Messiah, whose role is that of the suffering servant, who offers himself a ransom for many. Through his suffering messiahship, he creates a new humanity. In contrast, the classic ecclesiastical view is of God as male and of the Christ as the male image of God. In this traditional view, Jesus is a triumphal king and an authoritative High Priest. This traditional Christology has served to support a patriarchal religious consciousness in the church and in theology. Traditional theology has justified and guaranteed male dominance over women and the subordinate status of the female. The evil patriarchal order which subjugates and oppresses women in society is also seen to operate within the church. Women in the church are discriminated against and oppressed. But the suffering of the oppressed women and the solidarity struggle of those who seek freedom from oppressive patriarchal structures is participation in the messianic prophetic role of Jesus.[8]

4. The Mariology of AWRC:

In the Catholic Church, Mary's exaltation has been used to reinforce women's oppression while in the Protestant churches the rejection of Mary has oppressed women. It is therefore urgent that all Christian women take up the task of redefining Mary.[9]

— The real meaning of the virgin birth is that the human male is excluded from the birth of Christ.
— The end of patriarchy is announced.
— The glorification of Mary's perpetual virginity hinders Mary's access to ordinary women. No ordinary woman can be both virgin and mother simultaneously.
— Mary's saying "Thy will be done" is her motherly teaching of this same response to her son. Jesus says these same words in the Garden of Gethsemane.
— The words of the Magnificat announce complete change in the present patriarchal order (this means moral, social, political, economic and cultural reversals).
— Mary is in line with the great women in Israel.
— Mary's womb was the place of action of the Holy Spirit.
— Mary is the mother of suffering of the struggling people of the Asia-Pacific region.
— Feminist Mariology is a liberation theology which gives hope for humanization to all the world.

Christology and Mariology as seen by participants in the EATWOT and AWRC meetings have both commonalities and differences. Both criticize patriarchy and anticipate the new order. EATWOT theology tends to be more contextual, while AWRC follows the expressions of traditional theology more closely. The differences arise from historical context and theological orientation. It will be interesting to observe the development and changes in the same people's ideas on these subjects over the years.

In the years since the first EATWOT Asian women's conference and the first AWRC theological meeting, there have been many other meetings conducted by the two organizations. I would draw attention in particular to AWRC's work on interfaith dialogue from Asian women's perspectives. While every religion present in Asia has elements that oppress women, the strong feelings of many progressive male theologians in Asia against Western Christian mission policies and practice tend to lead them to emphasize only the positive in whatever traditional that we have. On the other hand, conservative Christians accuse those who take part in interfaith dialogue as syncretistic or unfaithful to the gospel. AWRC invites women from other religions and has a real dialogue, in which no one religion is placed above any other, but all religions are studied from the perspectives of women. To highlight the women's perspective, we have focused on three specific questions: (1) what is liberating for women in your religion? (2) what is oppressive for women in your religion? (3) what programmes or teachings in your religion might overcome this oppression?

Following meetings on these basic points in Kuala Lumpur in 1990 and Colombo in 1992, we now plan to move on to special issues, of which the first is violence against women and against nature. A meeting is planned for Kuala Lumpur in November 1994.

To conclude this section, let me mention the quarterly journal *In God's Image*, which serves as an ecumenical forum in which Asian women can express their realities, their struggles to be whole, their visions and their theological reflections. The contents include not only essays but also poems, prayers, liturgies and drama.

Individuals and organizations

To fill out this overview of how the EATWOT women's commission and AWRC have provided opportunities for women to come together to theologize and compare notes and experiences, I shall describe the works of several individuals and organizations in three countries: Korea, Philippines and India.

1. *Korea*

a. The *Korean Association of Women Theologians* (KAWT) was founded in 1980. It has 450 members, of whom 120 form an active core. One important feature since 1988 has been a correspondence course, in which about 200 women participate each year. There are two local chapters in Masan City and in Pusan. KAWT's objective is to unite women theologians and promote their development and, through the establishment of feminist theology, to contribute to the mission of the church and to build a just and peaceful society in Korea. Among its varied activities KAWT publishes a newsletter and collections of lectures and sermons; and every Wednesday the association is in charge of the half-hour radio programme "Good Morning, Ladies!", broadcast over the Christian network CBS.

b. Membership of the *Association of Feminist Theologians* is open only to those who hold a graduate degree (master and up) in theology.

The aim of this organization is to encourage research and publication by its members.

c. The *Asia Institute of Education for Feminist Theology* offers courses on biblical study based on feminist theology, feminist perspectives on church history and women's studies.

d. Most of the membership of *Christian Women for Democracy* is younger women, many of whom are active in the *minjung* (people's) church. Their basic orientation is anti-nuclear and anti-war, and they campaign for arms control, disarmament and the use of money now spent on the military for programmes to help women and children.

e. The *Institute of Feminist Theology* was established at Ewha Women's University to promote the renewal of Korean churches by working for women's liberation and structural changes through theological reflection on women's experiences and feminist-oriented reflection on Korean church traditions. To achieve this, the institute is engaged in academic studies, training and providing information and resources. Besides national seminars, it organizes international meetings in order to keep pace with the global discussions.

f. The *Christian Women's Institute for Peace* is engaged in studies on church and society and peace, seeking especially to articulate the role of Christian women in the process of Korean reunification. Its publication has 400 subscribers, and the institute has fifteen researchers. Activities include research, publication and lecture series.

g. *Korean Women Church* is a faith community begun by ecumenical church women and non-church women as a place to actualize partnership in relationships through experimental worship: community worship, drama, worship using the body and music.

h. *Story-telling Ministry* is a significant healing ministry among unfortunate children and women, encouraging them to tell their stories and listening to them.

i. The *Women's Commission* of the National Council of Churches in Korea works with representatives of the member churches. One of its priority concerns is the churches' participation in the process of national reunification. The NCCK has designated 1995, the fiftieth anniversary of both our liberation and the division between North and South, as a year of jubilee; and the women's commission is seriously engaged in the task of providing a feminist interpretation of the jubilee.

KAWT and other organizations publish several books each year, but since they are all in Korean they are little known outside the country. In 1990 Professor Chung Hyun Kyung of Ewha Women's University published a book in English, *Struggle To be the Sun Again*,[10] an insightful dissertation on feminist thinking in Asia and contextual approaches in Asian feminist theology. Currently, more than ten Korean women are enrolled in doctorate of ministry programmes at San Francisco Theological Seminary, all of them making attempts to articulate feminist perspectives. Their dissertations will appear in English.

2. *India*

The *Women's Institute for New Awakening* (WINA) is a Roman Catholic organization whose coordinator is Jessie Tellis-Nayak, a member of the advisory committee of *In God's Image*. WINA has many kinds of women's programmes, ranging from lectures on women's bodily functions to toy workshops to writers workshops. It also runs an annual course in feminist theology. Several members have written articles for *In God's Image*; of these I will mention just two: Stella Faria and Astrid Lobo Gajiwala.

Stella Faria, who is involved in both the EATWOT women's commission and AWRC, is an excellent theologian and author who writes straightforward Christian theology which she contextualizes by drawing on the Hindu background. Her article "Feminine Images of God in our Traditional Religions" (*In God's Image*, June 1989) is a study of how Hindu feminine images of God affect and influence women in contemporary society. The article focuses on Devadashi — temple prostitution.[11] Historically, such women enjoyed a certain prestige, but now they are just prostitutes, threatened and used by religious rhetoric.

In "My Marriage is Not a Sacrament" (*In God's Image*, Sept. 1990), Astrid Lobo Gajiwala reflected on her experiences after deciding to marry a Hindu, the agonies involved in negotiating with the Catholic Church and the support system she found among her friends. The church said her marriage could not be a sacrament because her partner was an "unbeliever", even though her husband told her he believes that Jesus is the Son of God, that marriage is an expression of God's love for God's creation and that the marriage ceremony is a sign of the total commitment of two persons to each other in the presence of God. She wrote to the Jesuit theologian Samuel Rayan, who said in a comforting reply that all who are committed to justice and human dignity and love for brothers and sisters are baptized, immersed in Christ's reality, the reality of God, and their love is the heart, life and meaning of all the sacraments. Although not a theologian by profession, Astrid Lobo Gajiwala raises very deep questions on practical theology that come up in the life-situation of an interfaith community.

3. *The Philippines*

The Philippines has the strongest national EATWOT women's chapter in Asia, due in large measure to capable leaders who were among the pioneers of the EATWOT women's commission. To prepare for the second Asian continental meeting, Filipinas held a national meeting in December 1992, at which 25 women of various backgrounds met to talk about violence against women under the theme "Spirituality for Life: Women Struggling Against Violence". The meeting included both sharing experiences and academic discourses presenting the subject in relation to indigenous culture, in relation to Islamic culture, from a psychological viewpoint and from a socio-political viewpoint. Virginia Fabella wrote up the conference report (published by *In God's Image*) in a way that vividly involved readers in the conference, with its use of group dynamics as well as individual intellectual capacity to bring the meeting to full bloom.

In conclusion, let me refer briefly to the work of two Catholic sisters who have given significant leadership to feminist theology in the Philippines, Asia and around the world. Mary John Mananzan has been very busy organizing the EATWOT women's commission's international meeting, in addition to her responsibilities in the Philippines. A short quotation shows the optimism and creativity of her writing:

> Spirituality is a process. It is not achieved once and for all. It does not become congealed. It is not even a smooth, continuous growth. There can be retrogression or quantum leaps. It has peaks and abysses. It has its agonies and its ecstasies. The emerging spirituality of women promises to be vibrant, liberating and colourful. Its direction and tendencies seem to open up to greater possibilities of life and freedom, and therefore to more and more opportunities to be truly, intensely and wholly alive![12]

I have already mentioned that Virginia Fabella is the major architect of the EATWOT women's commission, which was formed while she was the general secretary of EATWOT, and her book *Beyond Bonding* has been quoted often here.

In an essay on methodology in Christology, she mentions poor women's stories from the Philippines and Korea and says that "they are today the Christ disfigured in his passion".[13] Methodology, she says, should primarily be from the Asian women's perspective. Asian women must deal with their two disparate but interacting contexts: their Asian-ness and their woman-ness.

In order that knowledge of the context does not remain on a theoretical — or worse, mythical — level the theologians must be engaged in a "dialogue of life", not only with the poor who are mostly women, but also with those of other religious and cultural traditions and different ideological convictions. In this way, one develops an experiential understanding of the Asian context.[14]

A comprehensive analysis is a must in our doing of theology. Economic, political, religious, cultural and even ecological analyses are needed. The Judaeo-Christian scriptures are an indispensable source, but there is an urgent need to reread these from the woman's standpoint. Virginia Fabella does not preclude availing ourselves of the scriptures of other faiths as well.

That Jesus was male is not an issue for Asian women, for he is never seen as having used his maleness to oppress or to dominate women nor does his maleness necessarily lead to the conclusion that God is male. When we study our tradition, it must be re-examined and read anew from a women's perspective to distinguish between what contributes to women's emancipation and what leads to further enslavement.[15]

* * *

Asia is a vast continent, containing about half the world's population, diverse in language, religion and culture. Asian women make up about one-fourth of the world's population. Only about 3 percent of Asians are Christians.

Given these statistics, no one can really feel adequate when talking about Asian women's theology. In this short paper I have tried to depict the major streams, but many things have necessarily been left out.

Whether on the continental or national level or as individuals, more Asian women's voices need to be heard. We have to get out of our sense of excessive humility and our feelings of inadequacy and be bold enough to let our convictions be heard. We have to create a new myth for ourselves to replace the old one that Asian women are quiet and not forthcoming. Asian women are articulate and scientifically minded, while at the same time compassionate and passionate. We are creative and insightful. Let us encourage each other to be more productive and fruitful!

An accurate analysis of one's own situation is very important for theologizing; and an understanding of other people's situations is important for seeing why they are saying this or that. A lot of group work is now going on in Asian theological method. This is especially good in the starting stage. One thing to be clear about is that group work does not mean unison all the time. One should feel free to describe the pluralistic realities and thoughts of Asia.

NOTES

[1] Quoted by Barbara Sinclair Deckard, *The Women's Movement: Political, Socioeconomic, and Psychological Issues*, New York, Harper & Row, 1979, p.272.

[2] Virginia Fabella, M.M., *Beyond Bonding: A Third World Women's Theological Journey*, Manila, EATWOT, 1993, p.19.

[3] *Ibid.*, p.24.

[4] *Ibid.*, p.34.

[5] *Ibid.*, p.36.

[6] EATWOT Women's Commission, *Proceedings: Asian Women's Consultation, Manila, 21-30 November 1986*, p.130.

[7] *Ibid.*, p.154.

[8] AWRC, *Asian Women Doing Theology*, report from the Singapore conference, 20-29 November 1987, p.165.

[9] *Ibid.*, p.219.

[10] Chung Hyun Kyung, *Struggle To Be The Sun Again*, Maryknoll, NY, Orbis, 1990.

[11] Cf. Stella Faria and Sun Ai Park, eds, *The Temple Abused*, Seoul, AWRC, 1994.

[12] "Emerging Spirituality of Asian Women", in Virginia Fabella and Mercy Oduyoye, eds, *With Passion and Compassion*, Maryknoll, NY, Orbis, 1988, p.87.

[13] *Ibid.*, p.110.

[14] *Ibid.*, p.115.

[15] *Ibid.*, p.116.

An Asian Feminist Ecclesiology

MARLENE PERERA

Feminist or women's theology in Asia expresses the experience of our encounter with God and God's saving action in our struggle for liberation from all the fetters that enchain our people and us as women and prevent us from achieving our humanity to the fullest. The struggle of our women is an integral part of our people's movements and has social, cultural, political and ecological dimensions. Since the majority of our people are non-Christians, there is inevitably within these movements a dialogue of life, building solidarity and reciprocally challenging our beliefs and ways of being. Envisioning ecclesiology from this perspective, I would define its task as three-fold: (1) providing a critique of the present ecclesial model or paradigm; (2) envisioning pluralist models and paradigms of being church; and (3) being involved in the praxis of being the new ecclesia.

The present ecclesial model
The main points to be critiqued in the present ecclesial model would be:

1. The well-defined clerical and lay structure, with specific roles backed by an abstract theology, which divides the people of God into superiors and inferiors and promotes relationships of power and domination.

2. The basis of the structure of the church on Western feudal and monarchical patterns, which sacralize the power of patriarchal, hierarchical authoritarianism with the illusion that these authorities alone possess God and God's saving action. This power too often stifles the breath of the living Spirit emerging from the people of God.

3. The overt or subtle proselytism exercised by the church in various parts of the world. In the context I would not hesitate to examine critically the concept of the "chosen people".

4. The "absolute theology" of the church that maintains white and male supremacy.

5. The collaboration of the church with evil and death-dealing powers in maintaining the status quo, and the support given by the church to colonialist, neo-colonialist, capitalist, imperialist forces in the world, as well as the fundamentalist and passive otherworldly attitudes which this fosters.

Such a church produces a ministry which is dualistic, power-oriented, ritual-centred, pastor- and not people-centred, and promotes private piety. Its focus is the church itself. In its decision-making processes this church discriminates against women, children and other unwanted peoples, rendering them voiceless and excluded. It covers up, ignores or finds a way to escape facing the burning day-to-day issues of violence, war, marginalization, elimination of women, thus participating in the perpetuation of violence.

New models and new praxis

I envisage church as people — women, men, children interacting together. I see not one church but a multiplicity of churches that have been baptized by and taken root in the different faces of numerous human communities, manifesting the richness of the face of the immanent God walking with us on this pilgrimage. In this perspective it is the local church in all its richness and weakness which enters into deep communion with other churches, thus manifesting another profound visage of God. Communion is their unity in diversity, and together they grow in maturity, wisdom and grace. The church then is truly the sacrament, the sign, the symbol of God's kingdom that is within us and is coming to be.

The essential characteristics of such a church would be:

— The church as small communities of faith with structures that promote openness, trust, sharing, caring, reconciliation, partnership in communion and common and mutual responsibility for one another, humanity, the earth and the cosmos, thus expressing the solidarity in creation.

— A listening church, listening to the people, to one another and to the Spirit in the day-to-day events in our world, and making choices with the wisdom that comes from being attuned to the life-giving Spirit within and among us.

— A prophetic voice in the wilderness — a church that firmly refuses to compromise with the evil and death-dealing powers of this world, and overcomes the greed for wealth and prestige.

— A church as salt and leaven. Thus it is not necessary for the church to be a large body. I cannot see that the majority of people in Asia would one day be Christians. Nor do I see the need for it.

This church understands that God's saving power manifests itself through the "little remnant" who is faithful and responsive to God's creative Spirit. It accepts that God's saving power also operates through other channels. Hence I see the local churches entering into respectful dialogue with other religions and ideologies, remaining open to being challenged by them and challenging them in turn, so that together they can be not merely a prophetic voice but also channels of God's wisdom and presence. I like a church that has the maturity to acknowledge its mistakes.

The good news which such a church preaches would be relative to the situation of evil that exists in the world, not an abstract dogma or theology. Such a church can give hope and joy to this world. It will evolve a variety of theologies in the course of its history yet remain life-centred. Its theology is expressed in the language and symbols of the communion from which it emerges.

The ministry of this church, being the community of persons who commit themselves to follow Jesus, is life-centred, service-oriented and determined by gifts and aptitudes rather than by statutes and accidents of gender. There is no hierarchy of ministries and tasks in this church. Any task that promotes life and the service of the community is equally valued. Decisions are made in community, and in this even the child has its due place. I envision a non-sexist, non-racist, non-classist church.

Such a church celebrates with joy, in symbol and song, in rite and dance, its own life and its hope of the new life to which it struggles to give birth.

We together with our people *are* the church. I see something of this church already struggling to be born. So we can hope, we can rejoice.

Could we not let go, could we not risk and venture out towards the promised land like Abraham, and bring that hope and joy into the different corners of our world?

Reflections on
European Feminist Theology

ISABELLE GRAESSLÉ

To address an issue from the "European point of view" is interesting,
but quite a challenge.[1] Where does Europe begin? Where does it end?
What countries are included? If we leave geography for history, the
ground is no more firm. If we raise the question of the destiny of Europe,
it is clear that nobody knows what will succeed the Europe of militant
colonial powers and the Europe of ideological divisions.

In other words, how do we define today the notion of European
identity? And where are the women in the picture, if they even have any
place? We should probably begin by saying that there is not *one*
European culture but rather different cultures *of Europe*, each shaped by
its particularities and called European out of a certain sense of history
and destiny. European history has always formed itself around major
crises, political and religious. As a matter of fact, Europe came out of
the rubble of three catastrophes: the fall of the Greek city-state, the
destruction of the Temple of Jerusalem and the collapse of the Roman
Empire.

When I look back on my own European journeys over the past few
years, a real mosaic comes to my mind:

— The light is very different from one place to another. It is very bright
and strong in the South; inundated by the sunlight, everything,
landscapes and people, is underlined. In the North, the light is clearer,
also smoother. In the Eastern part of Europe, I found the light
beautiful, but quite different again: very oriental, very yellow-
coloured.

— The churches are very different from each other. Born in Strasbourg,
well-known for its majestic and imposing cathedral, where women are
immobilized into statues of Eve and Mary, of wise and foolish
virgins, of the blind synagogue and the righteous church, I was

amazed in the Nordic countries by the *stave kirke*, the wooden churches built around the year 1000, so small that only the rich men could enter — the beggars and the women had to remain outside. And in the Byzantine monasteries of the East each stone bears a spirituality in which women are praised as saints, mystics and mothers of the people.

— Women also are very different from each other. During a European ecumenical conference I attended as a student chaplain, I had planned a day on which men and women would meet separately until the end of the afternoon. The women from the Nordic countries were severely critical of this, saying it was unnecessary since they had acquired equality, rights and recognition years ago. At another point in my life, I spent much time with Spanish families. In this often almost tribal society, I was frequently the only woman in the midst of men, caught in heavy discussions. To find the women of the community, I always had to go to the kitchen! During a recent trip to Romania, I constantly had the feeling of being in a culture completely different from mine. In the streets of Bucharest I saw women dressed Western-style, but also other more oriental-looking women, with skirts and trousers, sitting on horse-drawn carts.

These few small examples may sound familiar, but they are also a sign that there is no real European unity. Where will the Europeans find solidarity together? And for what purpose?

To turn now to the specific issue of Europe and feminism, as a French woman I was aware of and fascinated by the Latin branch of feminist studies. I read Simone de Beauvoir and Luce Irigaray. I knew that I was not born a woman but that I had to become one (which is a statement I could still agree with). But before going to the USA to study theology I had never actually heard of feminist theology.

There, after having experienced the death of a very close friend, I discovered that the only way for me not to reject the divine was to convert my personal masculine and very patriarchal perception of spirituality into more inclusive images.

I then wrote a short novel about angels, one of whom was Gabri*elle*, who was fed up with being understood for 2000 years as a male angel.

When I returned to Europe and presented my doctoral dissertation, in front of five old and grey men, one of them began his speech by commenting on the red dress I was wearing that day, suggesting that since I was "Little Red Riding Hood", he ought to play the role of the "Big Bad Wolf". I knew I was back in another world.

When I asked my home church, the Lutheran church of Alsace-Lorraine, for a ministerial appointment, I was informed of the rule that married women could not get a full-time job in the ministry, so that if they had children, they could stay at home to rear them. When I came to Geneva as a minister in 1987, I discovered a church in which I had the same salary and the same duties as my male colleagues. I was immediately accepted as a student chaplain. However, working in the field of theological research was quite a bit more difficult. I also discovered no woman had ever held one of the positions of power in the church, the *modérateur* of the *Compagnie des Pasteurs* (a function once held by John Calvin). When I was asked in 1993 to be a candidate for *modérateur*, I said No, as had other female colleagues before me: it requires too many changes in one's way of functioning to get into a typically masculine role.

I would now like to comment briefly on four specific areas from a European perspective: history, the academic world, the church and language.

History

A map of languages in Europe shows that all the minorities (for example, Celts, Basques, Hungarians) are on the fringes. Basically, the conquerors — the Normans, the Anglo-Saxons, the Romans — invaded all of Europe and pushed the ethnic and cultural minorities back to the fringes.

Moreover, the myth of a unique and united Europe is actually a sexist myth, since it was founded on the invisibility and exclusion of women. Perhaps the first European woman whose prophetic voice went unheeded was Cassandra, during the Trojan war. Her "madness" was to prophesy the destruction of a nation. She was not listened to, and the god Apollo condemned her as mad. Already then women were being denied in their specificity and their identity and enclosed within the patriarchal house, trapped in the image of the guilty Eve or of the witch or of the temptress.

If we look to philosophical and cultural developments in Europe, the position of the classical Greek philosophers is well known: Plato tolerated women but Aristotle excluded them from political life. What is less well known is the exclusively male orientation of the Renaissance and of the rationalism of the Enlightenment.

The French Revolution began by introducing the goddess Reason in the cathedral of Notre Dame in Paris. But Olympe de Gouges, who wrote a famous manifesto on the Rights of Women, was killed on the guillotine.

The romanticism of Goethe and Rousseau idealized and sentimentalized *the* woman, ignoring the suffering of real women.

In the 19th century the fracture between the public and the private was even more strongly marked: the feminine virtues of obedience and motherly tenderness were restricted to the arena of the household, while the public virtues of competition, struggles and efforts for success were seen as typically masculine.

Even one of the greatest achievements of the European myth, the liberal democratic system which has been exported to all the other parts of the world, was reserved for men and excluded women. When Simone de Beauvoir wrote *Le Deuxième Sexe* in 1943, she was not yet able to vote.

It is of course no single part of the system which is responsible for the situation of women. But one must admit that the experiences and resources of women have never been integrated into the European narrative. The European hero is the adventurer — from Ulysses the great navigator to the capitalist conquistadors of the 16th century to the directors of contemporary multinational corporations. This myth has produced a sedentary Penelope, submissive, waiting passively, without any self-consciousness or growth of her own subjectivity.

Christian theology played an important role in this limiting of women's subjectivity, restricting their participation in the social contract to their pregnancies. Christian society established by Constantine and later by Charlemagne sacrificed feminine subjectivity. Women became invisible and anonymous to retain a place in this social contract, in their time and in history, under fatherly authority, with God the Father as a supreme guarantee. What began as a "social necessity" received a theological justification: a whole system was built up out of monogamous marriage, the mystique of suffering in silence, sanctification through service and self-denial.

Christian theology has introduced into its system a twisted view of feminine sexuality, exemplified by the discourse on Mary, virgin and mother (although in some periods, as in the Middle Ages, the figure of Mary played a strong role for the self-consciousness of women). The worst expression of the denial of the female body in the European sexist myth was the witch-hunting at the end of the 15th century. The women burned — estimates of the number vary from 300,000 to several million — were single women and widows who had moved away from the social contract of sacrifice.

It is clear that Europeans have no justification for thinking of themselves as the elite of Christianity. European feminist solidarity with other parts of the world is quite a new idea, because the sexist mythology of Europe has prevented European women from discovering their own racism, their collusion in the oppression of women in other parts of the world.

In the current debate on the future of a renewed Europe there is a great danger of beginning again from the same centre, building anew from the old sexist concepts. The experiences of Eastern European women testify that many still have the feeling of walking in the wilderness of poverty and lost ideals without seeing a promised land.

As I said before, there never was a single European culture. It is another myth that European culture is represented only by the art of a Michelangelo or a Rembrandt, by the music of a Mozart, by the architecture of Gothic cathedrals, by the Shakespearean theatre. There was always a multi-cultural richness in the centre of Europe. Before the Romans came, before the Normans and the Vikings came, there was Celtic culture. And there were always women to express themselves in art and poetry. And when the times allowed them to speak, there were women who spoke of their relation to the divine, women mystics from Italy and the Netherlands, from England and France and Spain.

We are now rediscovering what Lavinia Byrne has called "The Hidden Tradition": the tradition of all the saints, mystics, nuns, finding new ways of defining the divine and talking about spiritual experiences, especially in the open space of the Middle Ages.

Specialists speak about several European cultural paradigms:
- the traditional hierarchical concept of the world, which was dominant until the French Revolution;
- the more democratic conception which prevailed in the 19th century;
- contemporary "post-modernism", a time of insecurity, a time of the individual and of particularism. After the utopian humanism of the Enlightenment has come a sceptical humanism, tolerant and minimalist. There is no longer *the* truth, only the expressions of individuals, without any common identity or universality.

One possible way to express the meaning of Europe today would be the answer of *responsibility*. If the culture of Europe were a culture of responsibility, based on the idea that people are responsible, we could move on from the sexist European myth to the visibility of all the actors in public life, especially of women. Liberal democracy is the empty triumph of the sexist myth of Europe. There is another possible voice: the voice of those who have no voice in the dominant stream of history.

The academic world

This is where I encounter the most difficulties — as a theologian, not as a minister. In France there are women professors in theology, but they are not specifically feminist. Some of my colleagues wish on the one hand not to forget men and to help conscientize them and on the other hand to promote a feminine but not a feminist voice. For them, being a woman is enough for doing theology in a different way.

I believe that one must support two or three fundamental principles of feminist theology, such as the criticism of the androcentric and misogynist views of patriarchal theology, but to have this recognized as an authentic religious message and an authentic expression of the will of God is quite difficult in the academic world.

We in the south of Europe tend to look enviously to the north, feeling that in Germany and the Scandinavian countries women have achieved this recognition. Yet whenever I meet German and Nordic women, they tell me that it is still very difficult to be taken seriously. Seminars in feminist theology are organized by lay academies and centres (I think, for example, of a seminar in the centre I am leading in Geneva, where I met many women disappointed by the church); but the men in the academic world still do not take us seriously. One French Protestant theologian, when he saw a new book by Elisabeth Schüssler Fiorenza, was heard to say, "At last, something serious!"

I also hear of women who are tired of trying to enter the academic system, tired of explaining the feminist reformulation of doing theology, tired of offering to patriarchal theology an inclusive, holistic interpretation and receiving no positive answer. This also explains why many women leave the church.

One of the major questions I ask myself is whether it is still worthwhile to try so hard to introduce feminist theology. Is it really useful to invest time and energy in order to be recognized, or should we instead work with grassroots people, especially women who do not have access to academic education?

The church

The past decade has been marked by the struggle for the ordination of women in churches that do not recognize it, for example the Church of England. These are visible battles, and they must continue.

There are also less obvious struggles, especially perhaps in those churches (like the Protestant Church in Geneva) where there is apparent equality of women and men. In 1988 the Geneva church supported the creation of an Ecumenical Decade group, composed of men and women, lay and ordained. In 1993 the synod of the church voted a mandate for this group and reaffirmed its recognition. But more recently when the church presented a list of the priorities and challenges to which it wishes to respond in the coming years, the goals of the Ecumenical Decade of Churches in Solidarity with Women were not included, and women have again become invisible.

On the question of what it means "to be the church", on the question of the evolution of the images of the church's ministries for the community as a whole, on the question of the recognition of the integrity and the dignity of women, there is still a long way to go.

Language

It is definitely difficult to introduce inclusive language in Latin tongues; for example, the feminine form of "pastor" in French is obtained by adding a silent "e" at the end of the word. This has now become the practice, but for a long time it led to mockery from colleagues, even women colleagues (which demonstrates the phenomenon of the disparagement of women by women themselves).

The word "feminism" is itself a difficult one. The archetype of a feminist is seen as un-feminine, radical and aggressive, which has nothing to do with the southern image of a woman, elegantly dressed and made up, arranged to please the images of women the men have and want. One of the tasks of the 1990s may well be to find a new paradigm for the word "feminism".

What can European feminist theology offer

1. European feminist theologians must oppose any notion of a "Fortress Europe", by looking East, by opening borders, by evoking such forgotten Christian ideas as sanctuary, hospitality and reconciliation. These concepts could be very pertinent in countries like the former Yugoslavia, where women have been raped in front of their husbands and their children to further a mediaeval war.

2. European feminist theologians have an ethical responsibility to make women visible and to unmask the institutional poverty of women, making clear where and how this is linked to European imperialist history. The difficulties faced by women, particularly of ethnic minority groups, in achieving educational success at all levels, the suffering caused by unjust marriage legislation and the masking of violence within marriage (one woman out of ten is battered in France) are all linked with the

invisibility of women within the fundamental patterns of European thought and the oppressive ideology it has inspired.

3. European feminist theologians can take courage from networking — for example, through the European Society of Women in Theological Research, committed to research and struggle at the institutional level, through the Ecumenical Forum of European Christian Women, through the Ecumenical Decade of Churches in Solidarity with Women, through the Women's World Day of Prayer.

4. European feminist theologians should explore the full extent of the potentials of the conciliar process for justice, peace and the integrity of creation (JPIC). A first European ecumenical assembly on these themes was sponsored in Basel in 1989 by the Conference of European Churches and the Council of European Catholic Bishops Conferences. It brought a great deal of hope to communities, groups and parishes; and the two bodies have now decided on a second such assembly, probably in 1997. I would urge all European women theologians to join this effort, and I would urge equal participation for women and men in all the structures for its preparation.

* * *

I must admit that I have few hopes that the churches will be able to overcome their own sexism and become instrumental in overcoming it elsewhere. So far I do not see them moving from exclusive practices and beliefs to inclusiveness, blocked as they are by institutions that are uncomfortable with change.

Any change will be painful, because the gifts and charisms of women remain unwanted. Encounters with established forces will also be painful, but necessary.

I still hope for a time when women are no longer strangers to the decision-making processes. I still hope that women will no longer be subjected to punishment when they hold different views, because I know, from experiencing the power which comes from the feminine divine, that we are no longer "much beloved daughters" who will keep silent in the church. I still hope that more and more women will come through the fundamental oppression of being viewed as seductresses who need to be controlled. I wish to see more and more women turning the other cheek to accept God's all-embracing instead of the prescriptions of patriarchy.

We have discerned alternative pathways that lead to the liberation of all; we have created new images for speaking about God; we have left the crisis of male monotheism behind us and started to cross borders, to break down lines of demarcation. We have searched for the lost coin, and I know we have found it.

NOTE

[1] Some parts of this text owe much to the 1993 *Yearbook of the European Society of Women in Theological Research* (especially the article by Catharina Halkes and the dialogue between Mary Grey and Jana Opocenska) and to the excellent *Introducing Feminist Theology*, by Lina Isherwood and Dorothea McEvan, Sheffield Academic Press, 1993.

Women in Peru:
Making the Invisible Visible

ROSANNA PANIZO

Peru is a microcosm of Latin America's multi-cultural society. So striking is the contrast between classes and ethnic groups that it is sometimes difficult to remember the unity of this country, which has in fact been in a state of war for fourteen years because of terrorism. Older than that, however, are the deprivation and poverty and misery we confront because of the unjust global economic structure. Poverty has many faces, but it is most evident in the 12 million out of Peru's 21 million people who try to survive under conditions of extreme poverty. The term "feminization of poverty" is also very appropriate to describe the situation in my country.

Given this severe and widespread poverty the high percentage of illiteracy among women is not surprising. Poor women have virtually no access to education at all, and there are very few women who have access to higher education, including theological schools. As a result, there are very few women theologians or pastors, and it is only very recently that a few women have been "professionally" theologizing from a women's perspective. At the same time, many women's groups are working on biblical studies, spirituality and liturgical celebrations, and at the same time questioning and challenging their denominational traditions. There is a growing second generation of Protestant women entering seminaries and theological schools with a more critical eye than their mothers.

Some achievements

Sociologist Virginia Vargas distinguishes three main streams of the Peruvian women's movement: a specifically feminist one; a "popular" one that has grown out of neighbourhood unions, local self-help organizations and other workers' groups; and a traditional one attached to churches and political parties. The feminist stream works in practical and theoretical ways towards abolishing the subordinate role of women. The popular stream starts with the traditional role of woman as mother and caretaker and expands this role into the public sphere. Thus individual and family activities become collective enterprises, as in the organization of community kitchens or programmes for better child nutrition. This part of the movement is mainly represented by women from the poor settlements around Lima and other large cities. The third stream emphasizes the need for women to hold positions of responsibility in churches, political parties and government offices. These three streams, of course, often merge or overlap. Although there is sometimes tension and lack of understanding, there is also excellent cooperation. Different women are simply trying, in different daily circumstances, to find within society some free space that can give them identity, the right to participate in democratic processes or strategies for sheer survival.

The theologizing we are doing in our region cannot be explained apart from this irruption of women as subjects in society and church. This movement has reshaped our social analysis, our perceptions of the world we live in and our theological thinking. As women theologians and pastors with our people we are also involved and committed within this movement; and I believe that the women's movement has reshaped the perception of the world and knowledge itself.

Numerous *encuentros* (gatherings), held with the assistance of partner institutions from the North, have nurtured our desire to organize different networks and organizations of women pastors, theologians and Bible scholars within an ecumenical framework. They also have provided non-formal theological education to women and have empowered women who work very isolated from one another. The relationship of education and elitism has helped us to redefine the concept of ordination. In general we have tried to be more inclusive in the convocation of women's gatherings, though we recognize that we also need to continue to do specialized work.

The visibility of women in our churches began with the specification in the "historic" denominations of "quotas" for women in decision-making bodies. This is a tradition that we have inherited, but because it was not the result of our own learning process, our mothers remained unaware that their presence made any difference in the decision-making process. As this process continues, it now involves not only the affirmation of the ordination of women in many churches but also exploration of the nature of ministry itself and questioning of what it means to be human, man and woman.

A development that I see as potentially very fruitful for theology is the revolution in sociology and anthropology that has just begun in the Latin American academic world. While this process is happening within what is still in many ways a patriarchal framework of producing culture and knowledge, it is continuing with the revolution of gender approaches in the production of knowledge. At this time in our history the classical social theories used by liberation theologies are not sufficient to explain the concrete social realm and the need to change the subordination of the women in Latin America. Thus, we need this new tool in our theologizing and pastoral work.

Through a gender approach we can criticize, for example, the way in which programmes of development and technology (including some which are supported by our partner churches and agencies) have increased the burden of responsibility for poor women living under the conditions of survival. A case in point is the organization of poor women in food programmes, extending the traditional domestic role of women in the neighbourhood organizations. The problem is that while the women shift from their private kitchens to a communal one, the men still remain outside the kitchen. This doubles or triples the workload of women and causes them to feel guilty for "leaving the house and the children by themselves". Indeed, a first generation of teenagers in poor areas under this programme said that now they missed their mothers as well as their fathers, who were already absent from the families. This is a very simple example of how the nurture and feeding of the members of society needs to be the responsibility of the whole society, not only women. But the fact that women are consigned to this role is dramatically reinforced by the sacrificial economic system which holds us captive.

Some challenges

The Andean region has a large indigenous population, and one of our major challenges has to do with indigenous women. There is an indigenous Protestant church in which women participate, but they remain largely invisible, although this varies from country to country. For example, in Bolivia the level of literacy and thus of visibility among Protestant women is higher than in Peru. In my work in theological education I have held workshops in the Andean provinces of Peru. When I arrived the first time I found that the participants were all men. When I asked where the women were, I was told that they do not know Spanish. In the Aymara and Quechua cultures women do not have access to Spanish, and few *mestizo* people speak Quechua or Aymara. So *mestizo* and indigenous women are isolated from one another by language. However, a new generation of indigenous young women is involved in theological education, and the challenge to them is to articulate a theological language within their culture.

Another enormous challenge for pastoral and theological work is the need for more profound and interdisciplinary reflection on human sexuality and corporality. If women's sexuality continues to be related only to procreation, we will go on being imprisoned by our biology, especially poor women who have no possibility to control it.

Theological education needs also to find new concepts and methods to make it accessible to women. Women have begun to appear as subjects of theologizing in Latin America in the past twenty years, but in my region it has been only in the past ten years. In this connection, it is also urgent to expand our theological dialogue. There are still large gaps among women from the various regions in Latin America, as well as between Latin American women and those from other parts of the South and women involved in prophetic movements and theologies in the North. Languages and church structures have been a barrier to this.

Finally, I think that we as women and as human beings have not been aggressive enough to discover the capacities, skills and power we have in ourselves. The history of our region shows that we have the power to make the invisible visible. It is our historical responsibility to see that this continues to happen.

Feminist Theology in Brazil

ROSÂNGELA SOARES DE OLIVEIRA

Between coconut palms and seagulls...
Images as one looks out to sea.
Waters which restore a body too easily spiritualized.
Tastes and smells which stimulate and strengthen our eyesight.
And the seagull swoops down to my hand and sips a drop of the dark
liquid which crystallizes my being.
All this brings to mind a woman of long ago whose life blood had been
ebbing away for many interminable years (Mark 5:25-34). For some her name
has not been preserved. Others call her Berenice.[1]

How does this woman regard herself? What words does her silence
speak? How does her crimson discharge of blood strengthen the dark
crystal water which flows on the ground beneath the bare feet of so many
other women? What hands does this woman have with which to reach out
and touch power?

I introduce this woman to make myself feel near to my own soil — so
as not to feel that I am speaking to myself as I write — and also to bring a
mutual friend into this context. This article will also introduce many other
women who have followed different or similar paths en route to becoming
historical subjects.

To share our theological journey in Brazil is not simply to talk about
ideas but to explore experiences and thoughts and sometimes even
existential, emotional and political conflicts. These are not the words of
individuals; although they do appear with their own thoughts, their
thinking is formed in networks, encounters, celebrations, studies and
briefings. This is practical and not academic knowledge.

I shall begin by mentioning encounters. In Latin America, encounters
are places where people build up their knowledge together, where experts
and ordinary people exchange knowledge, where experiences are shared,

where there is space for spirituality, for experiencing ecumenism and for coordinating political action. Sometimes they give a new direction to people's lives, form small support communities, weave tangled lives into the utopia of a new humankind. Then I shall examine some procedures and methods adopted by biblical experts to develop their feminist biblical hermeneutics and introduce Ivone Gebara's proposed new anthropology, which she sees as providing fresh foundations for a new humankind. Finally, I shall list some challenges which this process places before us as we approach the next century.

I have tried to refer to the most recent documents available, some not yet published, since I believe that some texts from the awakening of women's consciousness in the 1980s no longer engage with present reality.

How does this woman regard herself?

Where can one begin an account of women and theology in Latin America? Beatriz Melano Couch considers Sister Juana Inés de la Cruz, who lived in Mexico from 12 November 1651 to 17 April 1695, to have been "the first woman theologian in the Americas, both north and South".[2] She was a poet, author and mystic who engaged in theological debate and even criticized a sermon by Fr Antônio Vieira. Like Eve, she wanted all the knowledge that life and literature could give her. She thus entered a convent, though once inside had to give that up as a sign of her conversion! After all, who gives women the right to acquire knowledge?

Maria José Rosado Nunes asks what has become of the legacy of Sister Juana Inés in the 20th century.[3] She sees in the turbulence of the years from the 1960s to 1980s — military dictatorships and social movements, torture and human rights, political alienation and participation — a period of a massive mobilization of women. Theological discourse confronted the relation between faith and politics, ecumenism and youth. In the Roman Catholic Church ecclesial base communities formed and spread, finding their legitimation in liberation theology.

In the 1970s some Protestant churches (Methodist and Lutheran) decided to ordain women to the pastoral ministry. This was followed by a process of biblical, theological and pastoral reflection on the identity, dignity and ministry of women, in order to strengthen the experience gained in the church and other institutions by the first women to be ordained in Brazil. Between 1978 and 1985 there were five Encounters on the Pastoral Ministry of Women in the Methodist Church, and in 1994 we succeeded in reviving the practice and held a sixth encounter with some of the newer women pastors and theological students. Lutheran women pastors have also arranged similar gatherings. The simultaneous entry of women into theology has also been strengthened, energized, renewed and deepened by local, national and international encounters, both denominational and ecumenical.

The first Latin American Encounter on Theology from a Women's Perspective (Buenos Aires 1985) was a key moment in building a theoretical frame of reference.

As liberation theology from a women's standpoint, feminist theology begins with our concrete experience, with our being and acting, with our seeing and feeling, with our speaking and our silence.[4]

A second such encounter took place in 1993 in Brazil. Dealing with the themes of violence against women, the Bible, systematic theology, ethics and spirituality, the encounter noted the transition from a "theology from a women's standpoint" to a "feminist theology", in other words, the introduction of the category of analysis of gender, race and ethnicity, linked with class analysis, inherited from liberation theology. In a report of the encounter, Nancy Cardoso Pereira writes:

Elsa [Tamez] made us take off through the history of our hermeneutical flights: first, when we were flying on the wings of liberation theologians, content with affirming that the poor were the mediators of truth; then, when we took the risk of undertaking low-level flights, gaining a women's perspective; and the flight we are now together engaged on, no longer on the flight path of the male theologians, but, using our own wings, enquiring into the limits of the canon, exploring the firmament of the heavens. This is soaring innovative flight.[5]

To prepare Brazilian women theologians to take part in the first Latin American encounter, a group of them organized a national encounter, which has continued and expanded in various directions. This project is now called the Sophia Project: Women, Theology and Citizenship, and is presently organizing a fourth national encounter of women and theology.

The theoretical results of these encounters have stimulated reflection by many Brazilian women theologians who are now recognized internationally. The 1992 encounter, taking place during the year when the 500th anniversary of the evangelization and colonization of Latin America was observed, was devoted to women as a sign of conquest and resistance. Its most exciting result was our ecumenical experience with women of African, indigenous and gypsy religions. It was a meeting of equals —

women from different religious traditions sharing together, listening with respect to one another and celebrating the cosmos.

In the Roman Catholic Church the first groups for theological reflection or pastoral action arose out of black consciousness. In 1983 the Black Pastoral Workers was formed; in 1987, the Black Theology Groups; and in the 1990s, an ecumenical group of black women grew out of the Black Pastoral Workers. These women have come together in their own encounters, raising issues that link the experience of being a woman with the experience of being black in their quest for identity, taking theology as a frame of reference. Ana Maria Sales Placidino effectively describe our spiritual experience of encountering the black, feminine face of God:

> God is the God of Life, who gains strength within a context of death. God's action is intermingled with the action of God's people. God is like the woman who braids hair, who, as she braids the hair of the little girls, is keeping black culture alive... God is a hungry, abused, enslaved little girl. God is a young black woman, militant and sensitive to the pain of the age in which she is living...
>
> This vision of the God of Life was a silent thread running through the long years of suffering, resistance to black genocide, false liberation, distorted Christian evangelization and the poverty of the people. But the moment has arrived: what was conceived in the silence of the night is being born in the hubbub of the day![6]

The most recent interdisciplinary debate involving women theologians and women from the feminist movement is on theology and reproductive rights. Three seminars on ethics and reproductive rights have brought feminists and women theologians closer together, not only for political struggle but also to share their knowledge. This has been welcomed by many women who have secretly faced the issue of abortion, especially ordinary women.

In addition to these examples, many other networks and groups of women, generally ecumenical, have organized themselves to think and act on women's issues and women's identity. Even in the academic world, there are cells, courses and feminist lectureships to promote fresh thinking, a fresh paradigm, fresh methods, a new society — in short, a new humankind.

How does this woman regard herself? Her eyes are overflowing with hope, which has not faded even after having spent all her resources in the search for her body — her identity, her sexuality, her religion.

What words does her silence speak?

These encounters have provided an agenda for feminist theological thinking in Latin America. One key issue that can be singled out is biblical hermeneutics, which has gone through various stages in an attempt to recover the memory of women, from an initial stage in which individual women were given a high profile in salvation history, the struggle for liberation and the Jesus movement, to the point of seeking to identify the social processes of domination and resistance in which women are involved.

Here I shall present some statements and challenges from the work of three experts in feminist biblical hermeneutics in Brazil.

Tânia Mara Sampaio writes:

> It is not the task of feminist biblical hermeneutics to isolate woman as a being still hardly understood and absolutely devoid of power, and consequently the victim of unqualled discrimination which must now be rectified. The task is rather to explore the processes of domination and exploitation, in which women have hewn out for themselves their own niche of power through lengthy resistance. Because that is what happens in all social groups.[7]

Thus we are trying to get away from always working with the idea of woman as an eternal victim in social relations and make way instead for a perception of her power (or lack of power) to negotiate. This is not to deny that women are oppressed in relationships of domination, nor to reinforce the image of the idealized heroine who remains within the limits of patriarchal society.

Tânia's aim is to perceive the multiple relationships present in the biblical text and how they interact, so as to arrive at an understanding of the relation between the Bible and life. This is the key for her biblical hermeneutics.

Nancy Cardoso Pereira thinks feminist theology has the odour of the Bible about it:

> We no longer read the Bible with the eyes of tradition or of science, but abandoning our trust in them both, we allow our sense of smell to point us to the possibilities of discovering the memory of God's people, which does not reinforce the ecclesiastical and social mechanisms which oppress women.
>
> The whole Bible is redolent with women, even where they are not evident. We sense the word of God in the text and in life, aware that revelation lies in this dynamic of understanding and making sense. We approach the text enquiring about the context. We use the scientific tools available to investigate the languages and cultures embodied in the text. But

we do not cease to sniff at the text, to suspect it, even to reject it if it has a bad odour about it.

We re-create the text, not in itself, but in telling it we re-invent it beginning with ourselves, since we are the owners of our own noses![8]

While she gives a prominent position to the Bible in feminist theology, her approach is also radically critical — of her own tradition and of scientific knowledge. It completely rejects the claim that science is neutral and the only form of knowledge and of understanding reality. Why is this? Because both tradition and science are built upon dualistic patriarchal paradigms which have produced elaborate hierarchies and subordinated those who are different: men/women, white/black, adults/children, rich/poor, etc. Rationalism also downgraded ways of understanding reality culturally associated with women, such as intuition or feeling. It despised everyday life, especially home life and looking after children.

Criticism of these methods aims at introducing into hermeneutics the everyday life of contemporary women and of women in the biblical text. This hermeneutics does not limit itself to texts about women, but asks why they are absent from other texts, because even there it is possible to perceive them. Its authority is linked with the freedom to follow the scent of an interpretation which does not reaffirm, at any level whatever, structures which oppress women.

Silvia Regina de Lima Silva takes the experience of black people as her starting point in biblical hermeneutics:

> In the process of building their own history and the history of their faith, our people made their own interpretations of the Bible, created their hermeneutics and discovered interpretative keys which have enabled them to take the word of God, which had been manipulated and proclaimed by the colonists/evangelists as a justification and legitimation of the system of slavery, and transform it into a word of consolation and resistance in our pain (not merely alienation) and liberation.
>
> This enabled us to experience a faith not marked by the dualism which on the basis of one person's belief excludes that of another. Such a faith did not imply mere syncretism, as it is so easily classified. We are experiencing a faith of dialogue, encounter and respect. The word is not absent from the process. There is a particular way of "reading", of understanding the Bible which nourishes this experience.[9]

The starting point for a black biblical hermeneutics is the experience of black people, beginning with the slavery of the past and continuing up to the social, economic and religious discrimination of the present. As with feminist theology, experience is the place from which to understand our relation with the sacred.

To understand this religious experience in the black community certain skills are needed — seeing, listening, learning, bodily expression. These skills would lead to a spirituality which is the reverse of a method strictly speaking, as Silvia puts it. Even while being oppressed, Silvia suggests, this community was creating its own biblical hermeneutics, its own religious practices. Their secret was

to have discovered that this Bible itself is not The Word of God but A Word of God. This same God has addressed another Word to us, has spoken, and is speaking, to us through the Orixás, through the tradition of our ancestors. Words of equal value, which are evidence of the loving care of our God.[10]

Doing theology with the oppressed (black people or women) as one's starting point means having the freedom and authority to call in question all that we know as Christianity. But who confers that authority?

To understand and interpret the Bible and to do theology, one must take account of the patriarchal nature of biblical times. Criticism of patriarchy is found generally in Latin American women's theological writings, but those who have developed it to the highest degree are perhaps Ivone Gebara and some biblical experts in Brazil. It would be more correct to say that they have *overcome* patriarchy by identifying the epistemological break produced by introducing the category of gender.

Ivone asks why women are subordinate and what rationale determines this inferiority; and because she is also not satisfied with the answer that women are socially inferior, she produces a new anthropology, drawing on contributions from the feminist movement, which by seeking new relations between men and women is laying the foundations for a new humanity.

In her book *The Inconvenient Daughters of Eve*[11] Ivone takes four feminist criticisms of patriarchal anthropology as the basis for identifying elements of a new theological anthropology:

— a unitary anthropology, rather than the dualist anthropology which treats spirit and matter, men and women as opposites and incorporates the difference into an almost ontological hierarchy;
— an anthropology which reconciles body and mind;
— a multi-dimensional anthropology, in which different expressions of what is human are manifest;

— an anthropology of relationships, which places greater value on autonomy and interdependence between human beings, nature and the cosmos.

Translating this into theological language, Ivone proposes:[12]

— a unitary theology, which replaces the hierarchy of beings with a transcendence which reveals the absolute originality of each and the impossibility of reducing one being to another;

— a theological reconciliation between mind and body, that is, taking the human body — the body of woman, always with sinful associations, and the body of man — as a theological locus where the divine is manifested;

— a multi-dimensional theology, which apprehends the divine presence in the different dimensions of the human and the cosmos, as opposed to a one-dimensional theology, which sanctifies the male-centred vision of the world as established by God;

— a theology of relationships, which replaces the hierarchical model of dependence with an apprehension of the deep relationship existing between all beings. The dependence of one being on another is moral and not simply ontological.

...the dark crystal water...

What challenges does this put before us as we approach a new century? Let me enumerate six:

1. Feminine theology or feminist theology?

In Latin American theology there is still a certain ambivalence about the term "feminist theology". A similar hesitation about language can also be seen in women's movements in Latin America, in the light of the stigma attaching to feminist movements in the first world.

Some would contend that the strident tone of the word "feminist" does not ring true to the situation in Latin America, since it focuses too much on producing theology in opposition to the masculine way of doing theology. Others use the term because its militant tone identifies them with women's struggles for rights throughout the world.

This difficulty can be exemplified by the title of the Portuguese translation of Elizabeth Schüssler Fiorenza's book *In Memory of Her: A Feminist Theological Reconstruction of Christian Origins*. The Portuguese *As origens cristãs a partir da mulher — Uma nova hermenêutica* literally means "Christian origins beginning with women — a new hermeneutics". Does this imply a difficulty in using the term "feminist theology"? Or does it in fact indicate how difficult it is to acknowledge that women can make an independent contribution to human knowledge? In any case, the term "feminist theology" is being used more and more in Latin America, particularly to differentiate it from theology which is not in dialogue with the feminist movement or which does not accept feminism as capable of making a theoretical contribution.

2. Liberation theology or feminist theology?

Liberation theology heralded the emergence of new political and theological actors. Taking the poor as starting point led to involvement with social and popular movements, setting up pastoral work for solidarity and awareness-building and a fresh theological approach.

Women, realizing that in the midst of poverty there were poor women, set out to produce a theology with poor women as its starting point. This process attempted to give a high profile to women in the Bible, in history, in social struggles and in the church. At the beginning there was uncertainty about whether this implied a theology for the liberation of women — an issue explored by Elsa Tamez in interviews with Latin American women theologians in the late 1980s.

The 1990s seem to mark a "coming of age", in which we recognize that we must engage in criticism of liberation theology in the light of feminist theology, even if the contributions of each to the other have not been exhausted. Why has this issue been raised in various groups and organizations working with women?

First, because the feminist movement in Latin America has always been linked with the struggle for the rights of women. It was the feminist movement that has publicized the practice of violence against women in the home and taken action on questions of women's health, especially reproductive health.

Second, the feminist movement has developed concepts to enable us to understand women's identity and civic role and the social organization that holds them in subordination. Obviously, ideas and practices in this area are not always in harmony. There is quite an intense debate around the concept of patriarchy versus the concept of gender relations, allied with relations of class, race and ethnicity.

Third, a close relationship with women and their daily life has raised issues which are not only economic. On issues such as sexuality, abortion and contraception, traditional theology has been repressive and liberation theology does not yet know quite what to say. How can we continue to stand alongside women, with the image of woman as the protector of life because her body is the bearer of life, if we do not face the suffering and death of thousands of women in back-street abortions or of thousands of others who are sterilized?

3. Feminist theology and black theology

Black theology also emerged from within liberation theology. It was an attempt to state that there are not poor people in a generic sense, that people who are poor are also of a particular race or sex.

The theology of black women throws up issues and reinterpretations arising out of the history of the black community and the violation of their identity. The subject for discussion proposed by these women is political action and ecumenism. Why?

People's religion leaves its imprint on their identity, and in Latin America poor black people were prevented from fully expressing their religious tradition. It is very common in Brazil to associate African traditional religions with the devil, as something to be exorcised and erased from people's identity and from social life. Black theology groups, especially those of black women, attempt to overcome this prejudice by approaching African religions in order to get to know them, not out of curiosity but as an ecumenical undertaking.

In other words, they face up to the question of black social and cultural identity and attempt to overcome the discrimination against those who have chosen to follow those religions. They discuss afresh such theological ideas as God, evangelism, Bible, on the basis of how the black community has experienced them, and thus recover the community's memory of history and its struggles of resistance.

4. Spirituality and the body

A theology enclosed in the mind or in reason is a legacy from the past. We are afraid of the body and its language, ashamed of its power, fearful of its freedom. The challenge is to discover the body as an essential part of our being.

What would be the results of our theology if it came to us via the medium of the body — a body resurrected by pleasure — and not as the product of our guilt?

The black community has discovered the body as a means of worship. They celebrate with rhythm and movement. So also do the indigenous peoples in their culture.

The body is the locus of sex and the locus where the holy is manifest. It is the speech of everyday life, of affection and of dislike. It is the frontier between life and death. The theology which takes hold of the body gives it warmth.

5. Women's experience
These are as it were magical words present in feminist theology. Words begin with experience and return to it.

Popular groups have come to understand that if each woman tells her story and her experience, they will come across similarities and differences which will strengthen them sufficiently to break oppression. Telling one's story makes one aware of being a subject in history. From word to word, from tear to tear, from smile to smile, women are discovering themselves as resurrected bodies present in history.

Experience is the point of departure for theoretical investigation which is, as it were, a constant criticism of abstract universals unrelated to everyday life with its sweat, its smells, the dishes and the children!

6. New paradigms
Women are not a subject to be studied, nor a separate chapter: women are part of humankind. It is not enough to feminize the masculine, nor to superimpose one on the other.

The search for a new paradigm, which is being identified as analysis on the basis of the categories of gender, race and class, is relocating the tradition we have inherited. In other words, women and men in relationship are reshaping humankind, ecclesiology, theology, morality, a vision of the world — in short anthropology.

The integral relationship of women-men-cosmos is remaking the environment for our survival and spirituality.

Hands to reach out and touch power
The woman with the discharge of blood did not wish to speak a word. She was all silence — anonymous, stealthy, like the culture created for women. But she had power in her hands. Or was it Jesus who had it? She had the power of self-esteem. She was struggling for her life. She had the power of her faith. She confessed it publicly.

And her story, beginning with her hands, has been heard in all corners of the earth. Jesus recognized the strength of this woman.

Are we not this woman? And do we not know many other women like her? May we all be learners of that power!

NOTES

[1] Bárbara Huefner, "A mulher com hemorragia e a ressurreição da filha de Jairo (Mc 5:21-43)" (The woman with the discharge of blood and the raising of Jairus' daughter [Mark 5:21-43]), in Bárbara Huefner and Simei Monteiro, *Em busca da tradição perdida. O que esta mulher está fazendo aqui?* (In search of the lost tradition. What is this woman doing here?), São Bernardo do Campo, Editeo Imprensa Metodista, 1992, p.128, note 1.

[2] Cited by Maria José Fontelas Rosado Nunes, "De mulheres e de deuses" (On women and gods), in *Estudos Feministas*, Rio de Janeiro, CIEC-UFRJ, 1992, no. 0, pp.15-16.

[3] *Ibid.*, p.15.

[4] Extract from the final document of the encounter, quoted in Ana Maria Tepedino, "Mulher e Teologia" (Women and theology), in Huefner and Monteiro, *op. cit.*, p.29.

[5] *Conspirando: Latin American Review of Ecofeminism, Spirituality and Theology*, no. 7, March 1994, p.49.

[6] Silvia Regina de Lima Silva and Heitor Frisotti, *Grupo Ecumênico de Mulheres Negras... desafios à vista!* (Ecumenical Group of Black Women... Challenges in sight!), basic text for the Third National Encounter of Black Women Pastoral Workers, Salvador, 1992, photocopied text, p.6.

[7] Tânia Mara V. Sampaio, *O corpo excluido de sua dignidade. Uma proposta de leitura feminista de Oséias 4* (The body excluded from its dignity. A proposed feminist interpretation of Hosea 4), p.21.

[8] Nancy Cardoso Pereira, *Perfume derramado das feministas* (The perfume poured out by the feminists), São Paulo, March 1994, photocopied text, p.10. This paper was given at the Sixth Encounter of Women Pastors of the Methodist Church. Nancy takes the text of Matt. 26:7-13 as an interpretative key to describe the task of feminist theology.

[9] Silvia Regina de Lima Silva, *Há sapatos velhos que fazem calos nos pés* (There are old shoes that give you corns on your feet), Costa Rica, August 1993, xerox, p.3 (lecture given at the licentiate course at the Bible Seminary of Costa Rica. An attempt to interpret the Bible on the basis of the Afro-Latin American and Caribbean situation).

[10] *Ibid.*, p.9.

[11] Ivone Gebara, *As incômodas filhas de Eva na Igreja da América Latina* (The inconvenient daughters of Eve in the Latin American Church), São Paulo, Edições Paulinas, 1989, pp.12-16.

[12] *Ibid.*, pp.37-40.

Latin American Feminist Hermeneutics: A Retrospective

ELSA TAMEZ

In Latin America, feminist theology and hermeneutics have radically challenged theology, biblical hermeneutics and the church. The process we have gone through in the past fifteen years has been most fruitful. I use the word process deliberately, because in our experience, a hermeneutical approach is not something fixed once and for all, but something living, which must constantly respond to the challenges of social, economic and cultural reality. That reality, in which women are also active protagonists, demands a new word that is relevant to each significant event in the history of our peoples and to all the individual subjects who make that history.

We still believe that history is made by autonomous subjects; we refuse to believe that it is made by the mechanisms of the total market of neo-liberal capitalism and that there is nothing more to be done. We believe that today more than ever before women have a huge contribution to make in countering the widespread lack of faith that the world can be transformed and organized according to a more human and inclusive logic. In this spirit we women are one with the movement of black and indigenous peoples who offer a utopia and different alternatives for those who have little faith.

Three fairly clear stages can be observed in the development of feminist consciousness,[1] and this in turn has affected feminist biblical hermeneutics.

To set this process in context, I shall start with three Latin American ecumenical congresses of women theologians and biblical experts held at sufficiently long intervals to show these stages. The congresses took place in Mexico (1979), Buenos Aires (1985) and Rio de Janeiro (1993). Obviously, the important thing is not the congresses as such, but all the experiences and new inputs brought to them, which show what women are thinking and where they are going. Roughly speaking, each congress reflects the ferment of a decade — the 1970s, 1980s and 1990s. Other meetings of women theologians, pastors and teachers of theology confirm the course taken by this hermeneutical process.[2] In addition, numerous theological writings and re-readings of the Bible reflect the progress made in hermeneutical thinking.

It is important to recognize that the hermeneutical experiences of one decade do not cancel out those of another. Very often different, even conflicting experiences coexist, sometimes within the same person, because of the different levels of feminist awareness in the movements of Christian women and theologians working in the church and the pastoral work at the base in which women theologians are generally involved. Nor is one phase to be treated as more important than another.

The contributions of each decade respond to a particular situation. Consequently, in what follows I shall first mention the most important facts about the economic, political, church and theological context in Latin America and the relation to the secular feminist movement, then outline the development of the feminist awareness of women as the "hermeneutical subject" and how this approaches the biblical texts.

Feminist hermeneutics in the 1970s

1. *The context.* The 1970s was a period of intense activity in the parties of the left and the popular movements: peasants, workers, neighbourhood groups, women, solidarity groups of all kinds. The revolutionary struggles which originated in the 1960s continued, but now faced severe repression by governments, as military dictatorships seized power through coups d'état — in Uruguay in 1971, Bolivia in 1972, Chile in 1973, Peru in 1975, Argentina in 1976. In Central America there were already military regimes in Guatemala, Honduras and Nicaragua. Massacres, disappearances and torture of women and men became widespread.

Local Protestant communities emerged, seeking a new way to express their faith on the basis of a popular reading of the Bible, while in the Catholic Church there was an amazing upsurge of base church communities, also reading the Bible from the standpoint of the poor. At the beginning of the 1970s a new openness developed in the Catholic Church, initiated by the bishops' document at Medellín. Towards the end of the decade, however, attacks on the theology of liberation began. An experience of ecumenism developed out of practical commitment to the oppressed and the victims of the economic and political system championed by the dictatorships.

At this time the theology of liberation was defining its method (theology as critical reflection on praxis in a context of oppression) and assuming the poor as a theological locus. Its whole hermeneutic and theology was worked out on the basis of the option for the poor. The fundamental themes, in addition to theological method, were the Exodus, the captivity and the historical Jesus. This was a time of political and theological militancy by Christian men and women.

2. *Building feminist consciousness in theology.* Women biblical specialists and theologians took the line of liberation theology. Gradually this led women to discover themselves as historical subjects who were oppressed and discriminated against, but also capable of liberation and theological production. This was of fundamental importance as a first step towards raising feminist consciousness. Women began to demand a special place for themselves as actors within the wider struggle for the liberation of society.

Theological work by women asserts that women must engage in a double struggle: on the one hand specifically as women, and on the other for the economic and political liberation of society. It stresses that this struggle must be linked to and simultaneous with the struggle for global liberation, rejecting any suggestion that one or the other can be relegated to second place.

In this phase the ideological polarization was such that there was practically no dialogue with Latin American feminist movements, much less with feminists in the first world. In general, the feminists rejected religion and mistrusted the women theologians, while the women theologians rejected any feminist demands that were not linked to the overall economic liberation of society. Nevertheless, some groups of Christian feminists did contribute greatly to establishing dialogue and breaking down mutual prejudices.

3. *Hermeneutics from the starting point of women's oppression.* At this stage, when the emphasis was on militancy in politics, theology and the church, women's reading of the Bible was also popular and militant, intended to be liberating and transforming. The starting point was God as liberator, in solidarity with men and women who were oppressed. The choice of texts was selective: only texts which spoke of liberation were chosen and applied to the doubly oppressed situation of women. The hermeneutical approach drew on the theology of liberation, focusing on the Exodus and the Christology of the historical Jesus, because of their

practice of justice. It was stated that women were implicitly part of the category of the poor, so that the option for the poor meant the option for poor women.

Thematic lines centred on re-reading and study of the biblical stories of women leaders (such as Deborah and Mary), women helping towards liberation (the midwives of Egypt), women who are never listed among the outstanding personalities of salvation history because they are unimportant and poor (like Hagar, a woman oppressed because of her class, her race and her sex) and, at a time of military cruelty and torture, the sacrifice of innocent women (for example, Jephthah's daughter and the Levite's concubine).

The hermeneutic tended towards a call to solidarity with the whole people, especially women who are doubly or triply oppressed. All the readings of the Bible were marked by a strong note of hope in a new society based on economic equality and new relations between men and women.

4. *Inclusive language*. At this stage there was little awareness of inclusive language. God was generally referred to as masculine. Although Christian women connected with the feminist movements pointed out the incongruity of this, their call evoked no response among the women in the theological world. Nor did they use the word "feminist", which was stigmatized as something foreign.

Feminist hermeneutics in the 1980s

By 1985 in Buenos Aires a different way of approaching the Bible was already evident. More women had come forward as active producers of theology. A certain uneasiness was beginning to be felt in the re-reading of the Bible and production of theology by women, a sense that it was no longer enough for biblical experts to affirm that women are implicitly included in the category of the poor. The poor have a face and a colour of their own, as well as a particular worldview which also conditions theological discourse. Women did not give up theological reflection on the struggle for solidarity and a life of dignity for all, but they added alongside it the need to read the Bible from the standpoint of women, because, they insisted, women have a double battle to fight: that of realizing their own human potential as women and that of achieving a life of dignity for all in a new society where everyone has enough to eat.

1. *The context*. From the political point of view, Central America had become the focal point of the continent, a ferment of popular organizations and armed groups fighting against dictatorships. The Sandinista

Front triumphed in Nicaragua, and other revolutionary movements in the region drew strength from it. The dictatorships in South America became increasingly discredited; one by one they fell and gave way to so-called "limited democracies".

As the Reagan administration in the United States moved away from the human rights policy pursued by the Carter administration, repression in the region grew worse. The right-wing Council for Inter-American Security in Washington published the Santa Fe documents I and II (1980 and 1988), in which clergy, theologians and base communities were specifically referred to as dangerous. It became clear at this time that foreign debt was draining the life-blood of our peoples. Economists and theologians worked together on a theology that sought to respond to the new economic and political situation on the basis of faith.

A very strong ideological polarization developed within the churches. On the Protestant side two organizations emerged which were at odds with one another — the Latin American Council of Churches (CLAI) and CONELA — while in the Catholic Church an aggressively repressive attitude developed towards liberation theology and theologians. The Vatican produced the famous document from the Congregation for the Doctrine of the Faith condemning the theology of liberation, and Brazilian theologian Leonardo Boff was summoned to Rome to give account of his views and was condemned to silence.

The theological themes dealt with reflected these experiences. They centred on the kingdom of God and human history, theology of life and theology of death, idolatry, discipleship of Christ, the spirituality of liberation and martyrdom. An open dialogue was started with liberation theologians on women and their theological work, out of a recognition that the problems were not a matter for women only, that the whole of society was affected by a situation of marginalization, so that all of us had to commit ourselves to that specific struggle, women being the principal protagonists.[3]

In the same year as the Buenos Aires meeting, 1985, a congress on black theology was held in Brazil. This decade was marked by the emergence of active movements of women, blacks and indigenous peoples; this was the dawning of indigenous theology.

2. *Building feminist consciousness in theology.* Women were becoming increasingly involved in theology. Considering themselves as active subjects of theology, they inevitably raised the concerns of women, even when that was not the specific issue under discussion. Theological discourse was perceived as highly androcentric and patriarchal; and

women wanted to see themselves represented in all theological discourse, not just when women were being talked about. They stressed that if theology is to be done from the standpoint of women's experience, the discourse must be different, because women's experiences and world-views are different from those of men, for cultural, biological and historical reasons.

Women theologians tried to reinstate the feminine in language about God. They challenged the traditional theological language as too analytical, rigid, excessively rational and word-centred; and they proposed new forms of theological speaking. Political praxis, they said, has to be accompanied by loving praxis to make it more human. The general nature of the option for the poor, with its emphasis on the economic level, was questioned. Many poetic discourses emerged, freely and unashamedly demanding to be recognized as theological. At the liturgical level the contribution of women was extremely innovative and creative.

It was at this time that dialogue and contact started with first world feminist theologians. But little was known and little use was made of gender theories.

3. *Hermeneutics from the standpoint of women.* Earlier, when the starting point was the oppression of women, priority was given to texts on women leaders and women who were oppressed. Now the concern shifted to work on the whole text from the woman's angle. The position of the woman who is doubly or triply oppressed was still central, but it was said that she had a specific contribution to make on the basis of her suffering and aspirations as a woman.

Women theologians and biblical experts worked on female images of God: God as mother and father. They sought to read the passion and resurrection of Jesus in the light of women's suffering and desire for liberation. The Holy Spirit, too, was seen as feminine. In short, they sought to feminize theology and the Triune God, claiming respect for the undervalued roles society has allocated to women. They insisted it was necessary not only to practise justice but also to show tenderness and loving solidarity, to comfort people who had been tortured, the mothers of people who had disappeared and women who were suffering. Men and women together should lovingly bind the wounds of all the persecuted people of the continent.

Three aspects of biblical work are worthy of mention:

• The search for greater freedom in our way of speaking about God, which was considered to be rigid and androcentric. The texts were worked on with great freedom, and an effort was made to reassert the value of everyday life and the dimension of pleasure and fun.

• Affirmation of the value of virtues such as motherliness, unselfishness and tenderness, which society has assigned to women and which had not been considered important in prevailing theories of knowledge. Under this heading they studied texts on resistance out of suffering and assigned a liberating dimension to commitment and sacrifice.

• Hermeneutical advances in the treatment of the biblical texts. In the past, only passages on liberation had been selected, especially from Exodus, the prophets and the gospels. In this phase they began to tackle the patriarchal texts that discriminate against women. On the one hand, they rejected readings of the texts which often made them much more patriarchal than they actually are, re-reading them to highlight the elements favourable to women. On the other hand — and this was a leap forward — when the text did not allow a re-interpretation, it was classed as non-normative. They refused to accept that God was willing to exclude any of his creatures. The hermeneutical approach here consisted in giving priority to the Spirit over the letter. Through the discernment of the Spirit they went against the letter, in order to be more faithful to the gospel.

Now the hermeneutical contributions of women biblical experts and theologians in the United States and Europe began to fall on fertile ground in Latin America. It was considered necessary to have a bold and daring hermeneutic which proposed to make a reconstruction of the text. They tried to transcend the text, to read between the lines and analyze elements which would enable them to reinterpret the writing or reconstruct it on the basis of criticism of the patriarchal vision and extra-biblical materials which shed light on a different reality hidden by the text. This way of treating the Bible raised the question of the meaning of the authority and inspiration of the Bible as the written Word of God.

4. *Inclusive language.* This phase saw the start of self-education in inclusive language, stimulated by the women of the Christian feminist movement, who began timidly to speak of God as mother and father, he or she — not yet in a generalized way, but nevertheless to an increasing degree.

Although the term "feminist" was not accepted in all circles, there was more tolerance and the word began to be used to characterize theology from the standpoint of women; "feminist theology", "women's theology", and "theology from the viewpoint of women" were used interchangeably. There was also talk of "reading the Bible through women's eyes".

Feminist hermeneutics in the 1990s

This latest phase started in a context which favours reconstructing all paradigms. It uses a radical, anti-patriarchal hermeneutical approach to propose a new, inclusive and non-patriarchal theology. The Rio meeting in December 1993 highlighted this new concern of Latin American feminist hermeneutics. The theologian Ivone Gebara proposes the total reconstruction of theology and calls this phase "holistic ecofeminism".[4]

1. *The context.* Internationally, the collapse of communist governments in Eastern Europe and the Gulf War shook many leaders of left-wing parties and the popular movements. In Latin America the decade started with the harrowing memory of the November 1989 massacre of six Jesuits and two innocent women in El Salvador, which was perceived as a symbol of Christians crushed because of their struggle for justice and life. Another event present in everyone's mind was the armed invasion of Panama by US troops. In addition, the Sandinista Front in Nicaragua lost the elections.

The new neo-liberal capitalist international economic order was being consolidated. The ideology of the total market, demanding constant economic adjustments, was presented as the only viable alternative; and the resulting privatization excluded more and more of the population. Women were the first victims. The aim was the dismantling of the state and opposition to its role of caring for the sectors in greatest need.

As a result of this political and economic situation the popular movement as a whole was greatly weakened. An exception was Haiti, where Jean-Baptiste Aristide was elected president in December 1990, but he was then forced into exile by a military coup less than a year later. In the church, the base communities stagnated and a major ecclesial crisis developed in several Protestant churches in various countries. At the same time, the end of the cold war reduced the ideological-political tensions and polarization within the churches. The amazing growth of Pentecostalism continued.

The Latin American Catholic bishops held their 1992 conference in Santo Domingo on the theme of "new evangelization", but the final document lacked the bite of earlier pronouncements. The Protestants met in Quito for the CLADE III congress. Neither gathering made any significant statements concerning women; indeed, the Santo Domingo document includes statements which are actually against women's realizing their status as autonomous subjects.

In this situation of despair and pessimism the indigenous movement emerged very strongly, asserting itself on the occasion of the 500th anniversary of European conquest as a new actor offering important theological and spiritual input. Indigenous theologians of different nationalities from all over the continent have already met for three congresses in the 1990s. In this context the women's movement and the black movement have also gained in strength, providing radical input and challenges to Christian theology and hermeneutics.

The theology of liberation focuses on various themes — the market economy and god of sacrifice, the new evangelization. Some theologians are working on the revelation of God in other religions, ecology, grace (over against the law, which enslaves). The urgent theme for many is that of hope or utopia. New doers of theology are demanding that the theology of liberation's "option for the poor" should become — in the words of the indigenous theologian Aiban Wawa — "the option for the impoverished other"; in other words, that the dimension of otherness should be taken into account as well as the economic aspect. New questions are arising, such as the relation of the masses to committed Christians and the role of the middle classes, to which little attention has been given in the past.

2. *Building feminist consciousness in theology.* In the previous phase a considerable variety of work was done on the female face of God and of theology. But there came a point when reflection could go no further. The sense of uneasiness about theological output has resurfaced. For a good number of women theologians it is not enough to speak of the female face of God and the Trinity. They recognize on the one hand that the values they have been using are often those which have been imposed as feminine but correspond to a false identity, and on the other hand that they are still working within the parameters of patriarchal theological discourse, even if it has been feminized. Ivone Gebara, who is in the forefront of this phase, with new theological propositions and language, points out that what we have been doing is patriarchal feminist theology. And indeed, Christian theological discourse is androcentric and patriarchal. The task is to reconstruct the whole of theology.

Most recently, Latin American women theologians and biblical experts have been stressing the importance of working on theories of gender, with a view to developing feminist theological discourse and biblical hermeneutics in earnest. Whereas the theology of liberation used economics and sociology to analyze the situation of oppression before going on to construct a theological discourse, women will have to use gender theories to make a serious analysis of the oppressed situation of women. At the same time black and indigenous women doing theology are also asking that anthropological theories and symbolics be used. In short, these epistemological and methodological concerns are not easy to respond to, and the questions — the most interesting and important thing in this phase — are only just beginning to be asked.

3. *Feminist hermeneutics.* Among the new hermeneutical proposals is that of accepting the human body and everyday life as a hermeneutical category. Women theologians and biblical experts refuse to assume an attitude of martyrdom and commitment as characteristic of women and are striving for a non-sacrificial reading of redemption.

They are working on texts, such as the Song of Songs, which speak of celebration, joyfulness, enjoyment of physicality and sexuality. They are trying to work on Paul's texts with new epistemological parameters (his relationship with women as an epistemological criterion, for example). They are trying to use gender theories in the biblical analysis of any text; Hosea has been worked through in this way, for example.[5] Using sociological exegesis, they have tried to put a face to women who have no name, by reconstructing the text (for example, the women in Acts, by Ivone Richter Reimer).

All this is very new, and more progress has been made on raising questions than on concrete biblical work. We are aware of the radical nature of this challenge, which means reworking, or rather reinventing, the whole of Christian theology. There is difficulty in re-reading the great theological themes such as Christology, the Trinity and ecclesiology because of their androcentrism. It is recognized that the implications of reconstruction take us beyond orthodoxy.

4. *Inclusive language.* The term feminist has been adopted and efforts are being made to destigmatize it. It is proposed to refer to the divinity by non-gender-specific names such as infinite grace, mercy, or energy.

There has been an explicit link with feminist theorists in order to obtain input on gender theories, but always with the concern that this input be critically reviewed and adapted to the Latin American context. The basic question is how to link feminist hermeneutics and theology with the basic concerns of our poor peoples and the system of the market economy and its neo-liberal policies.

Coexistence of the three phases

We should reiterate that these three phases found among women theologians and biblical specialists in Latin America co-exist. There has not been a linear progression with each stage replacing the previous one. Elements of all three may even sometimes be found in pastoral practice and writings. Moreover, the latest, radically new phase is very much in its early stages. The women working on this phase have completed advanced academic theological studies. Nevertheless, almost all the theologians and biblical specialists have questions in their minds that point towards this phase, because of the growing uneasiness felt by women in working with a sacred book and a theological discourse that is patriarchal.

For many of us, prior to any advances at the intellectual and academic level, comes the claim on our solidarity by the many women whose lives are actually at risk, not only from violence against them but also from lack of food, housing, work and education. We feel an uneasiness working on the Bible from feminist angles sometimes far removed from the reality of growing exclusion produced by the neo-liberal economic system. Our black and indigenous women feminists understand this situation perfectly well, because they have to make the link with culture as well as the economy. Their contribution to feminist hermeneutics is extremely valuable.

At meetings of women theologians and biblical experts one deep and abiding concern is the danger of pressing ahead towards the total reconceptualization of Christian thinking on the basis of feminist consciousness, but leaving behind the women of the people. Popular women's spirituality has progressed towards a less patriarchal conception of God, but God is always spoken of in entirely male terms. There is still a huge amount of work to be done at the base to help demasculinize the Christian God.

As in popular reading of the Bible, each biblical expert uses different exegetical methods. The hermeneutical circle is accepted, but feminist suspicion is also applied to the text and the context.

A basic general concern in hermeneutics is to understand the economic, political and cultural moment at which the text was written. There have been recent innovations here from attempts to combine input from sociological exegesis and theories of gender. For understanding the written text some women biblical specialists also use elements of structuralism. Higher criticism is used only when it helps to make a coherent presentation of the biblical analysis.

Great creativity is evident in presentation: besides analytical biblical studies we find meditations and poetic reflections of great biblical-theological depth, symbolically rich combinations of liturgy and biblical reflection and excellent Biblio-dramas in which the whole community can assume the role of biblical personalities, bringing in their own current concerns. Generally the same content can be presented using different modes as appropriate at the popular, intermediate and academic levels.

* * *

Latin American feminist hermeneutics emerged about 15 years ago. The focal points of the work on the texts have shifted in keeping with the major historical, economic and political periods in the continent and the progress in building feminist consciousness.

Various entry points have nourished and consolidated feminist awareness. One has been the struggle of women for decent material living conditions for all, in which they often discover themselves as dignified autonomous beings and begin to make the connection between the global and the feminist struggle. Another entry point has been through Christian women in organized women's groups linked with feminist movements. They have generally been the ones to call the attention of women Bible specialists and theologians to the need to take up the women's struggle. A third entry point has been the input of gender theory, with growing recognition of the need to know more about these theories and to discuss them in the light of our situation.

Added to this is the actual practice of women biblical experts and theologians as active producers of theology and in rereading the Bible; for there is a growing uneasiness with its treatment in Christian theological discourse, which is consistently androcentric and very often patriarchal. Similarly, given the serious economic and political situation in the continent and the challenge posed by the exclusion of a large part of the population through neo-liberal policies, there is also a certain uneasiness in working with radically feminist concepts in theological discourse without a clear, practical method to link economic, political, racial and feminist concerns.

We have seen three periods or phases in the study of biblical texts and theological discourse which have gradually appeared over the past three decades. The first phase corresponds to women's discovery of themselves as autonomous subjects: oppressed, capable of liberation and actively producing theology. The second phase attempted to rework biblical-theological discourse in the light of women's aspirations, suffering and spirituality, seeking to complete it with women's experience. The third phase is striving towards a new biblical-theological discourse with the help of gender theories; it is a question of deconstructing in order to reconstruct. In this most recent phase there are more questions and tentative proposals than fully worked out constructions.

The creativity demonstrated in liturgy, methods, content and modes of presentation is noteworthy. That is why we believe that women theologians, pastors, liturgical specialists and teachers of theology must work together.

NOTES

[1] I agree with Ivone Gebara, who speaks of three phases in theological discourse: "Aportes para una teología feminista", in *Tópicos '90*, Chile, 1993, pp. 71-133. For the first phase see also *Servir*, Mexico, Vol. 16 (1980), nos. 88-89; and *Comunidad de mujeres y hombres en la iglesia*, San José, SEBILA, 1981; for the second phase, *El rostro feminino de la teología*, San José, DEI, 1986. The first and second phases have been examined by Pilar Aquino in an outstanding study, *Nuestro clamor por la vida: Teología latinoamericana desde la perspectiva de la mujer*, San José, 1992. Very little material exists for the third phase but we may count especially on the input from Ivone Gebara's latest publications.

[2] E.g., two important meetings of women theologians and pastors with a large Protestant presence: one in San José, Costa Rica, in 1983 on the theme "Women and Men in the Church"; the other, under the auspices of CLAI, in Buenos Aires in 1989, which brought together more than 85 women pastors and theologians. At this latter meeting the proposal was made to found the Association of Women Theologians and Pastors of Latin America and the Caribbean. Also worth mentioning is the first encounter-workshop of women teachers of theology, held in February 1994 in San José, with the support of the WCC's Programme on Ecumenical Theological Education. These three congresses in fact correspond to each of the different phases mentioned here.

[3] Cf. Elsa Tamez, *Teologos de la liberación hablan sobre la mujer*, San José, DEI, 1986, and *Las mujeres toman la palabra*, 1989.

[4] *Op. cit.*, pp. 86-124.

[5] Cf. Tânia Sampaio, in *RIBLA*, No. 15, 1993.

Re-Imagining: A New Stage in US Feminist Theology

ELIZABETH BETTENHAUSEN

A milestone in feminist theology in the United States was marked in November 1993 by the Re-Imagining Conference in Minneapolis. Organized to celebrate the Ecumenical Decade of Churches in Solidarity with Women, the event brought together more than two thousand women and a few men for four days of ritual, renewal and reflection. This was the first primarily Protestant, ecumenical, national, clearly feminist women's gathering of this size in the United States, at least in this century.

A new stage in feminist theology

Several aspects of this conference seem to me to signal a possible new stage of feminist theology in the United States.

• One main purpose of the conference was indeed to re-imagine traditional doctrines of the church. Women approached this task with energy and passion born of the conviction that the survival of women and perhaps of the church depends on a theological revolution. To be vital and viable for the future, Christian theology will simply have to meet the requirements of women in very diverse circumstances and of all groups who have traditionally been subordinated or oppressed in a hierarchical system which privileges a certain male elite. The conference consistently attempted to overcome the separation of theology from social justice; and for the most part the differences and conflicts created by theologically guided struggles for justice were confronted rather than repressed or denied. While the majority of participants were Euro-American women, the speakers and liturgical leaders were more representative of the diversity of women in the world.

• A second purpose affected the import of strongly feminist presentations. As an early brochure put it, "thinking about God is not an exclusively professional experience". The conference provided an occasion for women from very diverse local situations to reflect theologically in small groups seated at round tables and to move back and forth between these small groups and hear the presentations in a larger group. In other words, what was heard from the "professionals" could be re-formed almost immediately through the particular experience of each woman and her small group.

• The women who planned the conference wove in a diversity of media, including non-verbal-painting, drawing and body-movement. I believe the effects of the re-imagined doctrines were thus embodied more richly than if they had registered solely as words in the verbal section of the brain. The room in which plenary sessions were held was a visual feast, with multi-cultural art works displayed throughout and new ones being created in ongoing response to the conference. Music played a central role, thus rooting the experiences in yet another part of each woman's mind-body.

• The planning groups made a serious effort not to fall into unjust appropriation of cultures different from those of the Euro-American majority. However, at times the presence of one or two women from another tradition seemed tokenism at best, and the attempts of Euro-American women to speak or sing within another tradition were often stilted. Nevertheless, the diversity of cultural and religious traditions manifested in the conference was a fourth important attempt to re-imagine the usually homogeneous expressions of faith by congregations in their all-too-often homogeneous, even segregated, local communities.

• The use of Sophia as the primary name of God was the fifth particularly noteworthy element. The development of "inclusive language" in US churches has largely been a movement to reduce the use of exclusively masculine terminology for human beings and to include girls and women explicitly in the language of scriptural translations, theology and worship. The reduction of idolatry in God-language has been much more difficult to achieve. In the 1980s the baptismal formula, "In the name of the Father, the Son and the Holy Spirit", was one primary location of this struggle. While many feminists then (and probably still now) used alternative trinitarian invocations, the exclusively masculine formula is still the official one for baptismal entry in the church in many denominations. The WCC's Faith and Order document *Baptism, Eucharist and Ministry* was no friend of feminism in this regard.

Thus when a major conference, with extensive press coverage, used a female name for God — usually without any "balancing" male designation — a significant step was taken for women (which is not to say that all women will welcome this) in churches in the United States. For women to call God by a female name over a period of days during a conference was bound to evoke and create an energy that was palpable and dangerous to patriarchy. This re-imagining was a bold move away from reactive reform to creatively re-imagining the most basic elements of Christian faith.

Yet, all this would not have raised the uproar it did without two more elements:

• The explicit and specific positive references to women's bodies in the context of worship made the break from patriarchy very clear. In the Sunday ritual of Milk and Honey (the eucharist was not celebrated, since many US denominations still prohibit communing with persons from other denominations), this litany of blessing was used:

Our maker Sophia, we are women in your image:
With the hot blood of our wombs we give form to new life.
With the courage of our convictions we pour out our life blood for justice.

RESPONSE: *Sophia Creator God, Let your milk and honey flow. Sophia Creator God, shower us with your love.*

Our mother Sophia, we are women in your image:
With the milk of our breasts we suckle the children.
With the knowledge of our hearts we feed humanity.

RESPONSE...

Our sweet Sophia, we are women in your image:
With nectar between our thighs we invite a lover. We birth a child; with our warm body fluids we remind the world of its pleasures and sensations.

RESPONSE...

Our guide, Sophia, we are women in your image:
With our moist mouths we kiss away a tear, we smile encouragement. With the honey of wisdom in our mouths, we prophecy a full humanity to all the peoples.

RESPONSE...

Women's bodies were active in ritual, not suppressed as they are in so much Euro-American Protestant worship. Certainly not all women at the conference felt comfortable with this actively embodied meeting, worshipping, sensual celebrating. Rising out of the stasis of repression cannot be effected in a weekend. However, for many women the celebration of women's bodies felt like coming home after a long, dry, hard journey.

• For some women at the conference coming home also involved coming out, for the first time publicly identifying and affirming themselves as lesbian. In a very moving ritual (emotionally and physically), these women joined other lesbian, bisexual and transsexual women in a large circle in the centre of the conference hall. The other women thus surrounded them, making lesbians and bisexual and transsexual women — so often forced to the margin or beyond the margin of the church — the centre of this celebrative session. Some of the speakers were also women whose lesbian or bisexual identity is integral to their theology. This final element of the conference served to remove any ambiguity which could possibly linger. This meeting was definitely a re-imagining of orthodox heterosexist ecclesiology.

A gift and a challenge
The invitational brochure for the conference stated, "We will gather 'our stuff' and offer it as a gift and a challenge to the church to engage in the struggle for justice, with and for women at the grassroots."

In several respects, then, women's experiences as assembled and created in the conference are indeed a gift and a challenge to the church. Women re-imagined traditional doctrines of the church in ways conducive to women's well-being. Women addressing the conference were distinctively, gloriously diverse, and many strongly named the sins of racism. Women from very different local situations engaged in theological reflecting in small groups, creating ecumenical women's theology. Women used a wide variety of art and cultural media to present a broad spectrum of cultural and religious traditions. Women called on Sophia. Women called forth women's own bodies in worship. Women affirmed women-loving-women.

This conference was open to anyone who wanted to register, although the great demand and the limits of space prevented many from attending who had hoped to participate. The conference was truly "women assert-[ing] ourselves and our power", "women who do not need to stand around waiting for male approval", as Beverly Harrison wrote years ago:

> Mark this point well: It is never the mere presence of a woman, nor the image of women, nor heart of "femininity" that is the heart of misogyny. The core of misogyny, which has yet to be broken or even touched, is the reaction that occurs when women's concrete power is manifest, when we women live and act as full and adequate persons in our own right.[1]

Indeed, the reaction by ultra-conservative interest groups within several denominations signalled the extent of the challenge which this concrete power poses. Calls for dismissing denominational staff women who had recommended funding the conference or participated in it were spread as fast as electronic mail and right-wing newsletters could send them. Charges of blasphemy and heresy abound.

In response to the often vicious reaction, a group of United Methodist women, including bishops, addressed a statement to their church in February, "A Time of Hope — A Time of Threat". It calls to account those who, "frightened by fresh theological insights and by challenges to narrow orthodoxy, are attempting to discredit and malign women". Naming this period of fresh theology carefully, they wrote, "Today's 'reformation' holds the potential for life-giving renewal in the United Methodist Church and in the hearts and lives of women and men alike." By International Women's Day on 8 March, more than 800 women had signed this statement.

At issue in this conflict is whether male privilege and power are intrinsic to God in Christianity. As one irate reactor put it, the conference tried to "demasculinize" God. Another editorialist said that it "clearly repudiated the historic Christian doctrine that God cannot be contained within the confines of human gender". Apparently the universalized male gaze does not consider that exclusively masculine metaphors and names confine God to human gender. Gender becomes an issue only when feminine and female language is introduced.

Some perceive the challenge which female God-language poses as an heretical threat; indeed, one retired United Methodist bishop claimed that "no comparable heresy has appeared in the church in the last fifteen centuries". Such reactions assume the zero-sum theological game of tired orthodoxy. In this view, bipolar opposition is ontologically given, so that any power gained by women must be at the expense of men, any power exercised by whites must be at the expense of blacks, any power exercised by humans must be at the expense of God.

Feminist theologians in the United States have been doing scriptural and historical study which more accurately locates Sophia in the history of Judaism and Christianity. Already in 1979 Joan Chamberlain Engelsman analyzed the historical "expression and repression of Sophia" in *The Feminine Dimension of the Divine. In Memory of Her* (1983) by Elisabeth Schüssler Fiorenza developed more fully the analysis of the displacement of Sophia by Logos terminology in the Johannine texts. More recently Elizabeth Johnson has written a brilliant analysis of Sophia as a bridge between classical Christian doctrines of God and feminist theology: *She Who Is: The Mystery of God in Feminist Theological Discourse*, a good example of how feminist liberation theology and metaphysical analysis can combine to free theology of pseudo-orthodox idolatry.

Carole Fontaine's essay on Proverbs in *The Women's Bible Commentary* contains a very helpful discussion of the Woman Wisdom and Woman Folly pair and a pertinent reminder that all the scriptural material on Sophia is in the context of patriarchy. Here, too, a hermeneutic of suspicion is required — or perhaps we might as feminists now claim a "hermeneutic of sophistication". To be as wise as the serpent makes a great deal of sense if the serpent is the familiar of Sophia.

Atonement and violence

Women have also been struggling with the classical Christian theories of atonement, specifically in connection with the systemic and personal violence to which women have been subject in their particular circumstances. Delores S. Williams has written what is certain to survive as a classic theological text: *Sisters in the Wilderness: The Challenge of Womanist God-Talk* (1993). Williams studies the "coerced surrogacy" to which black women were subjected under slavery "in the areas of nurturance, field labour and sexuality" in the period before the US Civil War (1861-65) and the "voluntary" surrogacy in which they survived after the war when they were pressured "to choose to continue in two surrogate roles: that of substituting female power and energy for male power and energy and that of Mammy".[2] In conditions of slavery and white racism, black women were "struggling to survive", a history which Williams traces to its contemporary expression.

Given the experiences of black women in surrogacy roles in the United States, Williams then turns to the question of redemption in Christian theology:

> More often than not the theology in mainline Protestant churches (including African-American ones) teaches believers that sinful humankind has been redeemed because Jesus died on the cross in the place of humans, thereby taking human sin upon himself.
>
> In this sense Jesus represents the ultimate surrogate figure; he stands in the place of someone else: sinful humankind. Surrogacy, attached to this divine personage, thus takes on an aura of the sacred. It is therefore fitting and proper for black women to ask whether the image of a surrogate-God has salvific power for black women or whether this image supports and reinforces the exploitation that has accompanied their experience with surrogacy.[3]

Rejecting the interpretation which finds salvific value in oppression (crucifixion), Williams focuses on the "ministerial vision" of Jesus. The "salvific value of Jesus" for African-American women lies in his "life of resistance". In lucid theological summary, Williams writes:

> Humankind is, then, redeemed through Jesus' *ministerial* vision of life and not through his death. There is nothing divine in the blood of the cross. God does not intend black women's surrogacy experience. Neither can Christian faith affirm such an idea. Jesus did not come to be a surrogate. Jesus came for life, to show humans a perfect vision of ministerial relation that humans had very little knowledge of. As Christians, black women cannot forget the cross, but neither can they glorify it. To do so is to glorify suffering and to render their exploitation sacred. To do so is to glorify the sin of defilement.[4]

Williams challenges black liberation theologians to take the "survival/quality-of-life ethic" of African-American women as an integral aspect of men's theological work. Her book is a brilliant example of womanist re-imagining of traditional Christian categories using the experience of African-American women as the major source and norm. It is also important for white women in the United States. Using black women as surrogates is still an element of white racism to which all white women in the United States are socialized to a greater or lesser degree.

Here, however, I would raise a particular surrogacy role to which white Christian feminists have sometimes assigned black women. In an often well-intended attempt to be "inclusive" or "multi-cultural", white feminists in the 1980s turned to literature written by African-American women when they needed "women's experience" for their feminist theological base.

Two factors made this an instance of assigning black women to surrogacy roles rather than of cross-cultural, inter-racial interdependence. First, white feminist theologians selected from and universalized the experience recounted by black writers and assumed it as their own, without attention to the power differentials of white racism. Second, the experience of African-American women was often used *in place of* the specific naming of the experience of white Christian feminists *as white.* In this sense black women's experience substituted for the protected, unanalyzed experience of white women.

Recently, African-American, Latin, Asian American and especially Native women have been calling white women to account for this refusal to acknowledge difference. A healthy discussion of appropriation and reciprocity has begun to emerge. Susan Thistlethwaite's *Sex, Race, and God: Christian Feminism in Black and White* is a significant step by a white Christian feminist to analyze white women's theological reflecting as particular and not universal. In feminist theory, a series of studies of the meaning of whiteness has recently been published. White women have as much trouble specifying being white as men have specifying being male after centuries of universalizing their particular experience. A second major re-imagining of atonement theory arises out of the experience of sexual abuse and violence experienced by children and women of every racial-ethnic group. Marie Fortune at the Centre for the Prevention of Sexual and Domestic Violence and Mary Pellauer provided early feminist theological attention to the epidemic of violence against women and children in the United States. In 1986 Joy Bussert, in *Battered Women: From a Theology of Suffering to an Ethic of Empowerment*, drew attention to christological teaching which endangers women. Perhaps more than any other piece of feminist theological work, it was an essay by Joanne Carlson Brown and Rebecca Parker, "For God So Loved the World?", which opened up the connections between abuse and theology. They make the case that it is "contrary to the gospel to maintain that suffering is redemptive". However, they are also careful to name the historical reality which is painful in its specificity: "Christianity is an abusive theology that glorifies suffering."[5]

In the past two decades women, men and children have broken the silence concerning the most dangerous place in the United States: the family home. Victims of battering, sexual violence, abuse, incest and other forms of rape are refusing to keep silent, claiming their own power and so moving from victimization to surviving.

Just as the home was mythologized as safe, so, too, the church had been construed as a haven from a violent world. Sexual harassment, abuse and violence within the church have been not only ignored and suppressed but also theologically condoned for centuries. Now, however, courageous women and men have forced denomination after denomination to confront the abuse of power sexually by clergymen and priests. Sadly, only civil litigation has really forced the church hierarchy to confront this rot in the body of Christ.[6] Other feminist theologians are attending to the interdependence of theology and violence and the necessity of breaking that bond for the sake of liberation.[7]

Although so cursory a treatment can only hint at the exciting theological scholarship concerning the Jesus of history and the Christologies of the church, it does point to the likely direction of feminist, womanist and *mujerista* theologies at their most thoroughgoing and creative: theology must conform to the norm of women's well-being in the diverse, specific situations of women. For many men and some women in the churches, this is deeply threatening, for the norms of patriarchy are indeed challenged and, as found wanting, rejected.

Sexuality and power

While atonement theology promises to continue to be controversial territory, sexuality, violence, power and authority are combined in another area of US church life in combustible ways. Opposition to the ordination of lesbians and gay men to the ministry and exclusion of lesbians and gay men from church-recognized marriage is perhaps the last stand of traditional Christian patriarchy. Here, too, feminist theologians are opening up a future which promises to be more appropriate to the multiplicity of family forms in which real people live than the sacralized middle-class suburban unit, and more loving than the truly demonic homophobia which some Christians have recently been expressing.

Carter Heyward has been a pioneer not only in the matter of ordination of women in the Anglican communion but also in developing lesbian feminist Christian theology. Her book, *Touching Our Strength: The Erotic as Power and the Love of God* (1989), has encouraged and empowered other women to acknowledge the public construction and import of personal lesbian identity. Yet many more women, especially clergywomen, are constrained by church policy and social structures and prejudice to keep their bisexuality or lesbian identity secret.

On this point two recent works are especially noteworthy. Mary Hunt, in *Fierce Tenderness: A Feminist Theology of Friendship* (1991), takes up the problem of heterosexual monogamous family life as a key metaphor in Christian teaching. Her very helpful discussion raises many questions about the restrictions in patriarchal social systems on women's loving friendship with each other. The consequence of these restrictions for adequate political organizing by women in the Protestant denominations has been great indeed. More recently, one of the early evangelical feminists in the United States has published a "coming out" book. Virginia Ramey Mollenkott's *Sensuous Spirituality: Out from Fundamentalism* (1992), especially the chapter, "The Lesbian, Bisexual and Gay Community as Social Transformer", raises important options for renewing the church. In many denominations organizations of lesbians, bisexual persons and gay men and supporters are calling the church to account for its long tendency to identify patriarchal phallocentrism with the new community in Christ.

It is no accident that Molenkott uses the title "Sensuous Spirituality". Feminist theologies in the United States have been consistently theologies of embodiment, of concrete social location, of cultural-historical specificity (although Euro-American feminists are only slowing catching up here to African-American and Latina feminists), of daily experience. Flinging charges of paganism and heresy is a final attempt to maintain the European and Euro-American captivity of the church. The dualistic ontology and politics intrinsic to that captivity are symbolically and actually embodied in heterosexual monogamy as an economic, sexual and social system. That God would work through the sensuous love of lesbians certainly unlocks the prison door. That the gospel can be preached vitally by a gay man is indeed heretical to those who imagine God as the patriarchal head of a cosmic family.

The present moment in liberation movements in the United States is a testing of the spiritual vitality of the country's old-line churches. Since the European invasions, sexuality has always functioned as a religious touchstone. Thus it is no surprise that today, when some church members see their old-time religion declining and disappearing, the battle over the definition of the church and the gospel is fought by means of the actual and symbolic social and theological construction of sexuality. As Virginia Burrus has demonstrated so well, the defining of orthodoxy has often been in the script of women's bodies as text. Her analysis shows that "the definition and enforcement of communal and doctrinal boundaries" are often effected through sexual issues. Not only does orthodoxy get articulated in sexual terms, but women assert and develop their own spiritual and theological power by using their sexuality over against the orthodox norms.[8] One of the features of patriarchal structures is that sexuality has bearing on every aspect of life: political, economic, cultural and certainly ecclesial.

Looking ahead

Were I to imagine what issues will — or, more candidly, should — occupy the attention of Christian feminist theologians in the next millennium, my dreaming would involve the following rapid eye movement.

My experience at the Women's Theological Centre in Boston daily convinces me more deeply of the need always to keep in view the connections of racism and sexism and classism (and increasingly of anti-Semitism, heterosexism, able-bodied privilege, etc.). However, I am growing more aware of how difficult this is to do, not least because powerful forces in the United States actively and violently try to fragment this analysis. Of course, the consideration of sexism apart from racism is hardly an option for women of colour in the United States, nor the consideration of sexism apart from classism for low-income women. The challenge is thus to white, feminist Christians who are not poor to avoid the reduction of women's experience to our own privilege. To accept the challenge, which appears contrary to short- and even long-term comfort, is not automatic.

In some respects feminist theology is further along in the critical awareness of the globalization of all social systems than is the rest of US society. And feminist theological work, thanks in significant measure to women such as Letty Russell and Nelle Morton, has always been more ecumenical than parochial. I expect this will continue. In a major study of women's spirituality groups in the United States, *Defecting in Place: Women Claiming Responsibility for Their Own Spiritual Lives*, Miriam Therese Winter, Adair Lummis and Allison Stokes report on the alienation which many women, Protestant and Roman Catholic, feel from the church. While many women refuse to give up on their hopes and actions to make the church more hospitable to women's lives, their spiritual well-being is often obtained by crossing denominational lines in creating feminist spirituality groups to sustain them over the long haul.

Another evidence of ecumenical cooperation is present in the anthologies of feminist theology, ethics, biblical studies, sermons published nearly monthly. In particular, *The Women's Bible Commentary*, edited by Carol A. Newsom and Sharon H. Ringe, and a forthcoming feminist commentary edited by Elisabeth Schüssler Fiorenza are evidence of the eroding of denominational demarcation among women. Elizabeth Cady Stanton, editor of *The Woman's Bible*, a pioneering feminist exegetical work, would be pleased with the fruits of her planting nearly 100 years ago.

The greatest challenge to feminist theology will probably be political. A little success leaps to hand as an excuse to take a much-needed rest from the struggles. In a reflection on the study of women's spirituality groups, I wrote:

> The reform of long-lived institutions is dangerous work, for the temptation to see improvement is nearly irresistible. The temptation is to mistake political temporizing for hope, tokenism for acknowledgement of capability, smiling spite for collegiality and rhetorical rejection of abuse for an increase of justice.

The situation of clergywomen in the denominations is not improving in step with an increase in numbers. Only in rare cases is the power of women on seminary faculties significantly greater than it was ten years ago. Very few seminaries require feminist study for graduation. The feminist movement in society is affected not only by backlash but also by the prevailing wisdom that narrowly defined special interest politics is essential to effective politics. The social norm of autonomous individualism is especially strong in academic institutions and tends to erode what feminist solidarity has been developed in the past. On the other hand, solidarity at the expense of acknowledging real differences is intrinsically unstable in the long run and unjust at every distance.

The problems and successes stand together in the same grove. Were women in the United States to organize ourselves as a political power for feminism in the churches, and were we in so doing to join with organizations and communities of women from Canada and Mexico and countries further away, what a wonderful re-creating of the church that would be!

NOTES

[1] Beverly Harrison, "The Power of Anger in the Work of Love", in *Making the Connections: Essays in Feminist Social Ethics*, ed. Carol S. Robb, Boston, Beacon, 1986, p.5.

[2] Williams, *Sisters in the Wilderness*, Maryknoll, NY, Orbis, 1993, p.73.

[3] *Ibid.*, pp.161f.

[4] *Ibid.*, p.167.

[5] "For God So Loved the World?", in *Christianity, Patriarchy and Abuse*, eds Joanne Carlson Brown and Carole Bohn, New York, Pilgrim, 1989, p.26.

[6] See Marie Fortune, "Is Nothing Sacred? The Betrayal of the Ministerial and Teaching Relationship", *Journal of Feminist Studies in Religion*, Vol.10, No.1, Spring 1994.

[7] Cf. Rita Nakashima Brock, *Journeys by Heart: A Christology of Erotic Power*, 1991; Ruth C. Duck, *Gender and the Name of God*, New York, Pilgrim, 1991; and June Goudey, "Atonement Imagery and Eucharistic Praxis in the Reformed Tradition: A Feminist Critique" (doctoral dissertation, Boston University). Goudey skilfully connects feminist analysis of "a theology of fear" in traditional atonement theories and a feminist re-visioning of eucharistic liturgy. Not the least important aspect of her material is its rootedness in the church experience of real women.

[8] Virginia Burrus, "Word and Flesh: The Bodies and Sexuality of Ascetic Women in Christian Antiquity", *The Journal of Feminist Studies in Religion*, Vol. 10, No. 1, Spring 1994.

Reflections on White Feminist Theology in the United States

LETTY M. RUSSELL

In the 1960s, when I was working as a pastor in the East Harlem Protestant Parish in New York City, we used to sing an African American spiritual called "Rise, shine, shine, for thy light is a-comin'", whose first verse proclaimed:

This is the year of jubilee...
[And God] has set [the] people free...

This spiritual expressed the excitement of people engaged in the US civil rights struggle. Never mind that we had not overcome. At least we were on the way towards freedom!

Today we could sing the same words, "This is the year of jubilee", as a sign of God's liberating action in our lives and in the communities of women engaged in the struggle for the wholeness and full human dignity of all women together with all men. We know the experience of God's Spirit moving among us as an anticipation of God's new creation of freedom, justice and peace.

In such a moment of jubilee it may seem a rather sombre task to address "the state of feminist theology today". Yet such a presentation has at least the possibility of celebration because it indicates what we are learning about how God is present in our lives. For we have been set free to search out the life-giving aspects of gospel tradition and ministry, and to transform the death-dealing aspects of Christian faith and practice.

There is so much ferment of freedom among women in the world today that I can only give a few reflections on one small part of the world as I see it. In that part of the world, North America, we are about to celebrate the hundred-year jubilee of *The Woman's Bible*, published by Elizabeth Cady Stanton and nineteen other women in 1898. The current feminist movement began thirty years ago with the publication of Betty

Friedan's book *The Feminine Mystique*.[1] I published my own first feminist piece on the interpretation of the Bible in 1971 and my first feminist theology book in 1974.[2]

The best I can do is to reflect on what seem to me to be a few of the important areas of feminist theology as it is shared, taught and practised among feminists of faith in the US in solidarity with our sisters around the world. In this reflection I will mention five current areas of work, sharing first my hermeneutic of suspicion or interpretation of the problems in that area, and then my hermeneutic of commitment or interpretation of possible transformations of tradition out of a feminist commitment to solidarity in faith and struggle.

1. Our mothers' gardens

A major issue for women in the feminist movement is the relationship of our faith perspectives, actions and struggles to those of our mothers and grandmothers and to our family traditions. As we reflect on the struggles and on the faith of our mothers, we notice many types of weeds and beautiful plants in the metaphorical garden of their lives.

Patriarchal weeds. We try to understand the many ways our mothers and we ourselves were mistreated or restricted in our life choices as women, and we often come to layers and layers of pain that have been covered up by those who had to go on no matter what, so that the family could survive. From the perspective of feminist theology we begin to apply a hermeneutic of suspicion to the ways our mothers tried to guide us to make the culturally approved choices for our lives, yet to warn us of the difficulties ahead. We wonder why it is that our brothers were treated differently from how we were. We wonder why we were taught to separate ourselves from persons of different classes, races, tribes or nations. We wonder why our mothers seldom grew up to be artists, church leaders or theologians. And we begin to notice a key element in feminist theologies, that of analyzing the structures of patriarchy that divide, conquer and oppress women, and the religious thinking that reinforces those structures.

In speaking of patriarchy I mean a social construction of reality and thinking about reality that is based on domination of women and of all groups considered inferior because of their race, gender, class or sexual orientation. Women are caught in the patriarchal web of oppression by a construction of human sexuality and gender roles that assigns women their status according to the status of the men to whom they belong. The pattern of domination and subordination is reinforced by a dualist way of thinking that divides reality into opposing categories such as women/men, spirit/body, rich/poor, black/white, heterosexual/homosexual and then assigns inferior status, value, evil or sin to the non-dominant group in each pair.

This understanding of patriarchy is not against men, for both men and women live in and support patriarchy. But it is a recognition that in order to understand why women's reality is so full of contradictions between what we are taught and what we experience, we have to look at the social structures and the way of thinking that declare that it is normal, right and approved by God that women are created in the image of God yet less than human. From this assumption and this way of organizing society many addictive weeds of oppression are planted, watered and nourished.

It is because of patriarchy that feminist theologies have to be theologies that advocate the God-given full humanity of all women together with men. They critique as idolatrous all structures that dehumanize women's lives because they demean those created in God's image and do dishonour to God. There is no way that white, middle-class feminists can oppose patriarchy if they do not know how it looks in different parts of the world. And there is no way to advocate the liberation of women if they are not aware of how the mothers' gardens are blighted in different ways in different cultures. In Latin America patriarchy looks like machismo. In parts of Asia it frequently looks like Confucianism. In India it is casteism, while in Japan it is Shinto worship of the ancestors. In the West it also looks like racism, capitalism and imperialism. In each place we can learn from each other how it works as we join together to analyze the implications of class, race, gender, sexual orientation, disability and many other divisions used to dominate and subordinate both in church and society.

Life-giving plants. At the same time as feminist theologies seek to analyze the weeds of patriarchy and to find ways to create a new vision of partnership and the full humanity of women and men, they also help us apply a hermeneutic of commitment. The commitment is to carry on the faith and the traditions of our mothers' gardens that can provide strong and nourishing roots. Our suspicion is for the sake of finding out what those roots are and how they can be nourished in new ways.

This was the purpose of the book I shared in editing entitled *Inheriting Our Mothers' Gardens: Feminist Theology in Third World Perspective.*[3] Here womanists, mujeristas, Asian, African, Latin American and white North American feminists all joined to examine their own gardens and the way they shaped the growth of their own faith and theologies. Each group names its own theological insights and orders its own garden, yet the insight of each is essential for the continuation of feminist research about specific patriarchal structures that demean the full humanity of women.

This is also a cutting edge of feminist theologies today, the way they work at learning from one another both the meaning of critical analysis and suspicion about themselves and their own collusion with patriarchal structures, and the meaning of commitment and solidarity with women who are doubly and triply oppressed because of poverty, war, domestic violence, AIDS and so much more. Besides the World Council of Churches, an important contributor to this dialogue has been the women's commission meetings of the Ecumenical Association of Third World Theologians (EATWOT).[4]

2. The spiral of Sarah and Hagar

In facing the difficulty of developing a multi-cultural approach in feminist theologies that does justice to the experience of those women suffering multiple oppressions, feminist theologies have had to develop a theological method that is contextual yet articulates a commitment to do theology as good news for the oppressed and those who are most marginalized.

Classical theology. Developing such a method is forced on feminist and all types of liberation theologies because of the dominant patriarchal paradigm or thought pattern of theological education and scholarship, which defines "classical theology" as what has been written by white, male Eurocentric theologians. If someone from the third world or a woman speaks of the tradition in a different voice, their contribution is not heard because it is not derived from traditional doctrinal and credal formulations.

This way of thinking is largely linear and deductive, placing heavy stress on the received intellectual and philosophical traditions of the church. A hermeneutic of suspicion leads us to ask why a particular culture, methodology and group of people should dominate the thinking of many voiceless Christians worldwide. We wonder why it should legitimize the patriarchal understanding of those who control the life, structures and witness of the church.

Our suspicion also leads us to notice that it is not true that this theology is totally logical, objective and unbiased. In fact it comes out of the culture and bias of a particular time and place, and has practical implications for the way our lives are blighted by justification of violence against women, denial of ordination for women, persecution of gay and lesbian persons, just to name a few things.

Feminist/liberation theological method. A hermeneutic of commitment to include those who are most marginal as full members of church and society leads feminist and liberation theologians to build their theological methods on a commitment to join God in working to mend the groaning creation in all its parts. This work of mending includes designing ways to do theology that can include the input of those struggling against patriarchy towards a new vision of partnership.

It does not ask just about women's experience. It asks about the experience of women and men of faith who are struggling for the full humanity of all women and of all persons who are oppressed. This experience of faith and struggle leads us into a spiral of action/reflection as we act out what we have learned and thus gain new insights and questions for going around the spiral again and again. Out of that experience of women's faith and struggle the questions for the hermeneutic of suspicion are generated, and we begin to analyze the social and historical causes of the contradictions of these experiences.

Such critical analysis and suspicion generates the questions we address to the biblical and church traditions and helps us to ask new questions about the ways texts are understood and traditions interpreted. Thus, for instance, we do not even begin to understand the dynamics of the story of Hagar and Sarah (Gen. 16:1-16; 21:9-21) until we read it through the eyes of the Egyptian slave woman in her struggles for her son. Nor do we understand why Sarah can act as she does until we analyze the situation to discover that the problem in the story is not Sarah and Hagar, but Abraham and God and the patriarchal customs and worldview that lock the two women into a downward spiral of competition for the patriarchal crumbs.

Working to reinterpret this text as Phyllis Trible, Delores Williams, Renita Weems and Elsa Tamez have done leads to clues for transformation and for actions of imaginative and constructive repentance by those of us who find ourselves playing out the role of Sarah in contemporary society.[5] Perhaps working together and listening together may encourage us to use the spiral of Sarah and Hagar.

3. The women's Bible

Along with the development of global solidarity in the struggle against patriarchy and the use of the spiral method of theological reflection, feminist theologians in North America have focused a great deal of their scholarship and energies on reclaiming the Bible as a text that is not only as a "text of terror" for women, but also as a "women's Bible", able to be heard in its life-giving voice of Christ's solidarity with women in their struggles.

Authority of the Bible. The women who challenge the authority of the Bible are constantly in danger of being called heretics by those who understand that authority as residing in the changing words of a text that is permitted to be interpreted according to a pattern of predetermined doctrine. Feminist interpreters pay particular attention to the way the biblical literature was shaped by patriarchal culture, worldview and interpretation. Their starting point is a hermeneutic of suspicion about the patriarchal paradigm of reality buried in the texts. As Mary Ann Tolbert has said, "one must struggle against God as enemy assisted by God as helper, or one must defeat the Bible as patriarchal authority by using the Bible as liberator".[6]

Feminist scholars such as Mary Ann Tolbert, Phyllis Trible and Elisabeth Schüssler Fiorenza have raised the question of how one might depatriarchalize the scriptures. They ask if it is possible to work with them at all in a way that would not be dangerous to women's health. Depatriarchalizing is dangerous work, for failure invites continued rationalization of subordination, and of rape and violence against women. It is also risky because it questions much of the biblical teaching that has been a source of authority in our lives.

But this is exactly what the work is about, claiming the authority to interpret the scriptures for communities of faith and struggle.[7] Authority is understood, not as the power of a particular teaching or text to speak of God, but the power of a particular teaching or text to inspire consent to faith and love in a community that struggles to find the message of God's love in solidarity with those who have been marginalized and denied the full empowerment of that love.

The state of feminist hermeneutics. In spite of the great difficulty of wrestling with the texts, many of which remain texts of terror in women's lives, the hermeneutic of commitment has created a large group of women who will not abandon the Bible to patriarchy.

In fact, so much has been accomplished in this field that it is one of the cutting edges not only of feminist theologies, but also of other forms of biblical study and research. We are well into a second generation of such biblical scholars, many of whom have published their own volumes as well as contributing to the new *Women's Bible Commentary*, edited by Sharon Ringe and Carol Newsom, as the first comprehensive attempt to gather some of the fruits of feminist biblical scholarship on each book of the Bible.[8]

In the last twenty years so much has been accomplished in this field that it is impossible to keep up with the publications. For a recent course at Yale Divinity School on "feminist hermeneutics", I provided an eight-page bibliography including only the less technical material, and 19 of the books listed were published in 1989 alone.

4. Our bodies, ourselves

A fourth area of development in feminist theologies is that of a holistic spirituality that incorporates wholeness, health and bodies into an understanding of embodied spirituality. In the struggle to control our own bodies and to make decisions about our own lives women are opposed by a church that is afraid of human sexuality and refuses to discuss the relation of sexuality and spirituality except when the former is equated with lust and vice. At the same time it enforces what Adrienne Rich has called "compulsory heterosexuality", a cultural pattern of patriarchy that often leads to the use of women's sexuality as a commodity. Such an attitude does not want women who are unattached to any man, nor does it want men who do not do their share of the work in controlling women and producing progeny.

Rejecting dualism. Embodied spirituality rejects the dualisms and hierarchies of domination and subordination perpetuated by patriarchal thought and social systems. Suspicious of all either/or's, it specifically rejects the separation of body and spirit, of male and female, of freedom and structure.[9]

When body and spirit are separated, spirituality can be nurtured through religious ritual and observance, while at the same time no notice is taken of forms of injustice that do terrible things to persons' bodies through rape, starvation, disease, degradation and suffering of all kinds. Those who suffer are told to wait for their reward in heaven; those who do nothing to stop that suffering or who even perpetuate it manage to live out all the contradictions of a split consciousness.

When male and female are separated and thought of as radically different, women become objectified and commodified as objects to be used by the dominant males to whom they belong. Men are identified with the spiritual and mind aspect of the body/spirit split. Women are assigned to the inferior natural realm of body, which needs to be tamed and controlled, and assigned tasks of physical maintenance: cooking, cleaning, rearing children and the like.

Finally, the dualism of freedom and structure posits the importance of human freedom and responsibility in caring for others and for the earth, but then develops a structure of accountability that allows great freedom to privileged white males and provides restrictive regulations for the subordinate groups. Thus morality is based on an unjust double standard, and the focus on sexuality and women's bodies and their control obscures the contradictions of such unjust moralism. Such dualistic thinking and acting helps to perpetuate the domination of any oppressed and less powerful group through the over-regulation by those with the power that comes with gender, race, class and heterosexist privilege.

Choosing to be whole. Spirituality has to do with the direction, meaning and value we give to the totality of our experience. Our spirituality is reflected in the choices we make about life that give it meaning.[10]

A feminist understanding of spirituality is a non-dualistic or holistic understanding that affirms the full humanity of women together with men. I would describe this spirituality as "the practice of bodily, social, political and personal connectedness so that life comes together in a way that both transcends and includes the bits and pieces that make up our search for wholeness, freedom, relationality, and full human dignity".

A Christian feminist spirituality is one that finds the guidance and source of transcendence in the God of Jesus Christ, and guidance in our life choices through the story of the life, death and resurrection of Jesus. It makes connections not only to ourselves, to God and to the needs of the world, but also to that community of faith and struggle which seeks to live out the liberating story of Jesus of Nazareth day by day. But feminist spirituality is not necessarily Christian, and much work is being done with the combination of spiritualities from different religions and cultural forms. Some of this can be seen in the work of Chung Hyun Kyung, Carol Christ and Judith Plaskow.[11]

5. Eco-feminism

Eco-feminism is an issue that connects with several of the other themes I have discussed, as it rejects the patriarchal identification of women, bodies, matter and sin, as well as its dualism of spirit and matter, which allows for the rape of the earth and its domination by those who would exploit it for their own power and capital accumulation. It also recognizes the issues of ecology that interplay with issues of war, injustice, poverty, starvation, malnutrition and lack of health.

The rape of the earth. At a time when the ecological interdependence of the world is understood so clearly, and when scientists are warning us of the destruction of our own planet and its biosphere, we continue to see the rape of the earth by multinational corporations who clear-cut, strip-mine, kill whole bodies of water with pollution and move us towards nuclear disaster in order to produce cheap energy.

Women are joining with ecological movements in recognizing that this aspect of oppression and domination is intertwined with disregard for their well-being and that of their families. In many third world countries women are moving to put together all aspects of life into an interdependent ecological whole. The building of communities requires attention to resources, ecological balance and cooperation with nature as well as attention to the political structures of justice and peace.

Organic models of creation. At the same time theologians like Rosemary Radford Ruether and Sallie McFague are using the perspective of eco-feminism to locate their theology in a world context that seeks out wholeness and health for all by reinterpreting Christian traditions of domination.

Ruether seeks to reinterpret and transform the Christian traditions of creation in order to reject theologies of patriarchal domination in favour of a new formulation of covenantal and sacramental tradition that promotes the healing of the world.[12] She uses the tradition of Gaia, the earth goddess, as an image of the earth as a living interdependent system.

In the same way McFague highlights the shift in scientific understanding towards an organic understanding of the creation and then moves to reinterpret doctrines of human creation, God, Christology and eschatology in a way that is more consistent with this organic and interdependent understanding of the world as God's body.[13]

* * *

Do feminist theologies have a future? Is this truly a time for jubilee or some kind of wake in the face of growing violence against women and backlash all over the world? There are many advocates of patriarchy around the globe who would like to convince us that we are into "heresy" and "syncretism", as the furor over the Re-Imagining conference in Minneapolis in November 1993 amply demonstrates. We might celebrate the fact that US feminists have made so much progress that the 2000 women and 80 men singing and chanting in Minneapolis become a symbol of national threat to religion and family. But we also have to acknowledge that for most of us most of the time, it is neither jubilee nor wake. It is just struggling along, leaning on one another as sisters in the wilderness! Most of the time the second verse of "Rise, shine, for thy light is a-comin'" is more applicable:

Intend to shout and never stop...
Until I reach the mountain top...

NOTES

[1] Betty Friedan, *The Feminine Mystique*, New York, Norton, 1963.

[2] Letty M. Russell, *Women's Liberation in a Biblical Perspective*, New York, National Board YWCA and United Presbyterian Women, 1971; *Human Liberation in a Feminist Perspective: A Theology*, Philadelphia, Westminster, 1974.

[3] Letty M. Russell, Kwok Pui-Lan, Ada Maria Isasi-Diaz, Katie Geneva Cannon, eds, *Inheriting Our Mothers' Gardens*, Philadelphia, Westminster, 1988.

[4] Virginia Fabella and Mercy Oduyoye, *With Passion and Compassion*, Maryknoll, NY, Orbis, 1988; Virginia Fabella, *Beyond Bonding: A Third World Women's Theological Journey*, Manila, EATWOT and Institute of Women's Studies, 1993.

[5] Cf. Delores Williams, *Sisters in the Wilderness: The Challenge of Womanist God-Talk*, Maryknoll, NY, Orbis, 1993; Phyllis Trible, *Texts of Terror*, Philadelphia, Fortress, 1984; Elsa Tamez, "The Woman Who Complicated the History of Salvation", in *New Eyes for Reading*, eds John S. Pobee and Bärbel von Wartenberg-Potter, Geneva, WCC, 1986; Renita Weems, *Just a Sister Away*, San Diego, CA, LuraMedia, 1988. Other examples of suspicion about the way Christian traditions can be transformed include Elizabeth A. Johnson, *She Who Is: The Mystery of God in Feminist Discourse*, New York, Crossroad, 1993; Marjorie Proctor-Smith, *In Her Own Rite: Constructing Feminist Liturgical Tradition*, Nashville, Abingdon, 1990.

[6] Mary Ann Tolbert, "Defining the Problem", *Semeia 28: The Bible and Feminist Hermeneutics*, ed. M.A. Tolbert, Atlanta, Society for Biblical Literature, 1983, p.120.

[7] Cf. Letty M. Russell, *Church in the Round: Feminist Interpretation of the Church*, Louisville, Westminster, 1993, pp.38-39.

[8] Carol A. Newsom and Sharon H. Ringe, eds, *The Women's Bible Commentary*, Louisville, Westminster/John Knox, 1992.

[9] These three are spelled out in a 1991 report of the Presbyterian Church (USA) on human sexuality, "Keeping Body and Soul Together: Sexuality, Spirituality, and Social Justice", pp.28-31.

[10] Mary Hunt, "Spirituality for Creative Survival", tape A-1795, from Credence Cassettes, National Catholic Reporter Publishing Co., 1983; cf. Mary Hunt, *Fierce Tenderness: A Feminist Theology of Friendship*, New York, Crossroad, 1990.

[11] Chung Hyun Kyung, *Struggle To Be the Sun Again*, Maryknoll, NY, Orbis, 1990; Judith Plaskow and Carol P. Christ, eds, *Weaving the Visions: Patterns in Feminist Spirituality*, San Francisco, Harper & Row, 1989.

[12] *Gaia and God: An Ecofeminist Theology of Earth Healing*, San Francisco, Harper & Row, 1992.

[13] Sallie McFague, *The Body of God: An Ecological Theology*, Minneapolis, Fortress, 1993.

Womanist Theology

DELORES S. WILLIAMS

In this paper I shall describe the theological development in the United States called womanist theology by responding to three questions: (1) Why do black female theologians in the USA need a theology that is not named feminist theology or black liberation theology — even though it is inextricably related to both these theologies? (2) What social, cultural, political and theological factors have contributed to the development of womanist theology? (3) What have womanist theologians contributed to the Christian community's understanding of biblical hermeneutics, theological doctrine, ethics and the church's mission?

This paper presents my own views about the birth and development of womanist theology, and other womanist scholars in religious studies might differ with it, but I think all would agree that we are trying our very best to let the experience of black women speak to us and not to impose upon it vocabulary and ideas that come from beyond the cultures where black women live. This does not mean that womanist theology is done in isolation, without dialogue and learning from the analysis done by other women from different cultures. But African-American women's experience has its own integrity and must speak its own truth in its own language, expressing its own cultural ideas about women's reality.

When I was a graduate student at Union Theological Seminary in New York City, a group of Christian women from the black community of Harlem invited me to speak to them about feminism and feminist theology. When I finished speaking, one woman stood up and addressed me:

> Honey, I want to say something about this feminism... This all reminds me of the day I went into a fancy dress shop downtown and saw a real pretty dress. The colours in the dress blended right. The design was modern and fashionable. The buttons in front looked real pretty with the material. Everything

about that dress looked just right. There was only one problem... The dress was size five, and I wear size twenty. The saleslady told me that shop didn't carry no dresses over size thirteen. I can sew real good, but I knew there was no way for me to alter that dress and still have the same thing. There just wasn't enough material in that dress to make it fit me. Now that's my point, honey. This feminism and feminist theology is real pretty, but there just ain't enough in it to fit me. And what I'm wondering is: if you black feminists try to make it fit me, will you still have the same thing?[1]

This experience and a few others like it led me to concentrate my search for theological resources in the everyday lives of African-American women who live, work and die in the context of black community life.

One warm spring day I was walking with one of my white feminist friends, another graduate student, on 125th Street in Harlem. A young black man called to us, "Hey, pretty mammas, you looking good, looking good!" My friend instantly became angry. The young man was sexist, she said, assigning her to the maternal role women are always expected to fill. But I felt complimented by him, so I called back: "Right on, brother!" Then I explained to my friend why I was feeling complimented. "It is ancient folk knowledge in most African-American communities that black men love their mothers very much," I told her. "You can talk negatively about their fathers, but if you talk negatively about their mothers, you might get into trouble and a lot of pain. When the young man called us 'mammas', that was a friendly greeting, full of respect. He was telling us we are respectable, good-looking women. So I felt complimented and responded positively."

It was this incident and a few others like it which alerted me and my white feminist friend that there was a world of cultural difference between us, which was bound to make a difference in how we identified issues, experienced the world, even named ourselves and our reality.

These events made it clear to me that some women in the black community at the grassroots saw value in feminism and feminist theology but doubted that it was adaptable to their life-situation, and that there are cultural differences between black and white women's worlds that feminist perspectives might not be able to negotiate.

A new name

I believe there are five primary reasons that other black women have taken part in the new spelling of our theological name from "feminist" to "womanist" theologians.

1. There was tension between how African-American women defined women's experience and how they thought white feminists wanted black women's experience defined. In their understanding of women's experience, African-American women included both their struggle alongside all women in the women's rights movement and their experience with black men in the liberation struggle for all black Americans: females, males and children. Black sociologists such as Elsa Barkley Brown criticized white feminists for not wanting to include black women's racial experience as women's experience and for not wanting to include race among women's issues. Black liberation theologian Jacquelyn Grant also criticized white feminist theologians in the USA for not devoting time and energy to eradicating racism.[2]

2. Some black women had reservations about white feminist definitions of patriarchy as the primary cause of *all* the oppression *all* women experience. They doubted that this description had "enough material in it" to define adequately the kind of *systemic* oppression black women experience in the USA. They felt they needed a description that not only identified men as oppressive decision-makers and functionaries managing the systems controlling their lives but also was very clear about the participation of upper-class women with upper-class men in the exploitation of black women's labour, especially black female domestic workers. Most definitions of patriarchy provided in the USA were silent about white men and white women of every social class working together to maintain white supremacy and privilege.

African-American women who had travelled to other parts of the world saw that in countries where a light-skinned and a dark-skinned population live together, the former (female and male) usually oppress the latter. Black women discovered a global culture of whiteness that was systemic, perpetrated through every institution in such societies. Its language was racial, economic and cultural imperialism; its methodology the imposition of white Western order.

Black women did not know where white feminist women in the USA stood in relation to this global culture of white over black and white privilege, but many feared that the leadership in the feminist movement in church and society adhered to a prophesy made in 1903 by the southern US white feminist Belle Kearney:

> Just as surely as the North [of the USA] will be forced to turn to the South for the nation's salvation, just so surely will the South be compelled to look to its Anglo-Saxon women as the medium through which to retain the supremacy of the white race over the Africans.[3]

African-American women who had travelled around the world had discovered that there are many forms of "master and mistress" rule. Patriarchy is only one way for the powerful to control the powerless. In the African-American community there were also women who, with black men, participated in the oppression of other women. Black women needed additional language to name and describe the ways of "master and mistress" rule they had experienced over the years.

3. Many African-American women became womanist theologians because they needed their own theological voice to affirm different cultural foundations for identical assertions made by both feminists and black women who later became womanists. An example is Rosemary Radford Ruether's normative principle of the "full humanity of women". A womanist affirmation of this principle is based on a cultural foundation of black resistance that white American women neither have nor need.

Ruether's statement helps womanist theologians to resist the claim, heard continuously for more than a century in the USA, that black people are animals and not humans. Historian John David Smith's eleven-volume *Anti-Black Thought 1863-1925* (1993) is a collection of pamphlets circulated widely in the USA, which sought to prove that black people are not human. Of special interest are the selections in which white ministers and laypersons argued on biblical grounds that black people are beasts.

Since white women have not experienced such a continuous attack on their humanness based on their race, their affirmation of Ruether's principle could be based upon their resisting the more "elevated" accusation that women, because of their sex, are not in the image of God. This accusation was used in the church to support the subordination of women, but it was not used socially or by "Christian" leaders to define white women as beasts.

Black women were so defined; and so womanist theologians, in asserting "the full humanity of women", are resisting and denying a negative idea about all black humanity that prevails in the USA even to this day, in addition to resisting the contention that women are not in the image of God.

4. Living and working among the poor, some black women became womanist theologians as they struggled to do God-talk which emerged out of that social, cultural and historical context. They tried to produce theology whose construction, vocabulary and issues took seriously the everyday experience, language and spirituality of women. This kind of struggle needed its own theological ideas, framework and vocabulary.

5. African-American women could not limit their concern, definitions, struggles and goals to the survival, liberation and well-being of
women. The entire African-American family — mother, father, children
and black kinsfolk — was oppressed and confronted by systemic violence. Feminist observations about the growing "feminization of poverty"
were astute, but not much mention was made of the thousands of
homeless, jobless, poor black men and black families (fathers, mothers
and children) living on the streets of the USA. Nor was theological
attention being given to the violence destroying African-American communities — caused mostly by drug-trafficking, which is controlled by
non-black forces. Young black people, especially young black men, were
being killed at an alarmingly high rate. Numerous black women were
falling victims to drug addiction, and their rate of incarceration has
increased dramatically. Black people claimed the black family was under
siege by drugs and poverty. African-American women needed a theology
conscious of these facts at every moment. Black people's survival was at
risk, but no Christian theology (feminist and black liberation theologies
included) had made survival one of its primary issues.

Black women also needed a theology that was conscious of the sexism
in the African-American community. In 1979 Jacquelyn Grant wrote an
article in which she claimed that black women are "invisible in black
theology".

> In examining black theology it is necessary to make one of two assumptions:
> (1) either black women have no place in the enterprise, or (2) black men are
> capable of speaking for us. Both of these assumptions are false and need to be
> discarded. They arise out of a male-dominated culture which restricts women
> to certain areas of the society. In such a culture, men are given the warrant to
> speak for women on all matters of significance. It is no accident that all of the
> recognized black theologians are men.[4]

Other black female theologians began to recognize the qualitative
difference between the experience of black women and of black men even
though they both experienced racial oppression in the United States. My
own work discusses the uniqueness of black women's experience in terms
of the surrogacy roles they have been forced to fill from slavery to this
day. The surrogacy experience provides a different lens through which to
envision the task of womanist theology and provides different questions
to be asked about God's relation to the world.[5]

African-American female theologians could not separate racism and
sexism if they were to take seriously black women's experience in North

America. When this compound oppression determines the way black female theologians understand reality, they often imagine a whole new world and see issues differently from black male theologians. And since poor black women were a major concern for African-American female theologians, they also had to be attentive to a "triple oppression" affecting poor women's lives — race, sex and class.

Social and educational factors

As more black women were coming into seminaries for theological training at all levels, many were attempting to prepare for a vocation that brought together the parish and the academy, the practical and theoretical dimensions of Christian life. Women who had this double vision took the lead in "birthing" womanist theology.

Through community education, training in secular universities and seminary studies black women became acquainted with models of black female leaders from the past who had been active in community ministry even though they were refused ordination, among them Jarena Lee and Zilpha Elaw, who made a powerful impact upon the nineteenth-century societies in which they lived and worked. They became subjects of their histories rather than objects people used, and they told in spiritual autobiographies of mystical encounters with God that changed their lives and sustained their activism in the community.[6] The work of Lee, Elaw and other unordained black women represents early manifestations of "The Church Without Walls", which has become the metaphor for the work of lay, grassroots womanist theologians like Betty Bolden (described later in this essay).

Acquaintance with these nineteenth-century foremothers gave twentieth-century black women the inspiration and faith that they could also be effective community agents for social change. They could work simultaneously for black people's rights and for women's rights. God would give them strength just as God had given their foremothers strength for the struggle.

The second wave of feminism in the USA, beginning in the late 1960s, focused society's attention on the oppression of women. This movement inspired women to become more self-conscious, more aware of their own needs, aspirations and cultural resources, which had been buried by generations of male domination. Some secular groups of black women began to move away from a total affirmation of themselves as "communal selves" ("We are, therefore I am") to a realization of the need for "individuation", a clearly delineated *female* self apart from a peoplehood self. Yet they wanted their individuated female selves to be in harmony with and to participate in black people's collective struggle for liberation, survival and well-being.

The African-American social and cultural revolutions of the 1950s and 1960s had emphasized a communal way of thinking and acting which obscured black women's oppression and black male sexism. The emphasis was on black liberation, articulated and led by black men who gave little or no thought to black women's issues or their absence from leadership roles in the struggle. The second wave of feminism gave some black women a public forum in which to articulate their experiences of oppression, isolation and violation.

Secular black female scholars, influenced by the feminist movement, began to uncover African-American women's imaginative literature and history, including the work of black female theologians who considered their religion to be a power-source sustaining their activism. The writings of nineteenth-century black women like Ida Wells Barnett, Mary Church Terrell, Anna Julia Cooper and Maria Stewart were resurrected from obscurity and became sources for theological reflection, helping to pave the way for the birth of womanist theology.

A significant cultural factor, which provided the name "womanist" and some important clues for the development of womanist theology, is the work of the African-American poet and novelist Alice Walker. The word "womanist" appeared in the title of her book *In Search of Our Mother's Gardens: Womanist Prose*, published in 1983. Not only did Walker's definition of a womanist[7] accomplish what feminist and black theologians had not — to provide an image of black women's experience in their works — but she also offered tools for the analysis of culture in the United States, so that black women's culture, experience and history could be lifted from obscurity into visibility. At last black female theologians found some of the "material needed" — in the words of the black woman in the story I began with — to make a theology of women's experience which "fit" black women.

Walker provides an introduction to black womanhood that affirms mothers and children and is grounded in African-American culture. She situates her definition of a womanist in a family context: a mother giving advice to her female child. Inasmuch as the father is not mentioned, one can assume that this may be a single-parent family like so many black families in the USA. Walker describes the characteristics of a womanist (which also includes the mother) as being serious and being in charge.

She provides an anthropology of black womanhood as she stresses black women's culture, emotional flexibility and their love for themselves, for the folks, for art, music, dance, food and for the spirit. In the area of sexuality she advocates sexual preference for women. She defines a womanist as affirming roundness — a female body-type prevalent among black women, especially the poor, but stigmatized by the advertising industry as undesirable. She takes away the negativity associated with skin colour, which has caused so much racism and pain for African-American women. In womanist culture, colour becomes a universal reality in which all people participate biologically. No colour is better than another, and the value of persons is not based on the colour of their skin.

Her definition also refers to female leadership of black people's freedom movements in the United States. Those who know African-American history know that her reference to the liberation struggle points to a black female liberator of slaves in the nineteenth century, Harriet Tubman, herself a runaway slave who was called the "Moses" of her people.

To express the qualitative difference between "womanist" and "feminist", Walker writes: "womanist is to feminist as purple to lavender." One of the most important themes in her definition is survival: a womanist is "committed to the survival and wholeness of an entire people, male and female".

Walker's definition describes how "we African-American women are culturally" across class boundaries. She is careful not to emphasize higher education, which often establishes a black elite class no longer able to communicate with black people who do not have university education.

Walker has provided the cultural themes womanist theologians needed to unearth black women's experience and history embedded deeply in androcentric US culture, white and black. These cultural themes are: family, with female relationships emphasized; single-parenthood; women's intellectual pursuit ("wanting to know more than is thought good for a female child to know"); "colourism", which is the foundation of racism; women's leadership roles; women's resistance patterns; the objects of women's love (the folks, food, roundness, nature, dance, hospitality, men, women and the spirit); sexual preference; women's community work with men in survival and liberation struggles; the organic relation between womanist and feminist.

Theological factors and cultural themes

Various womanist theologians have been influenced by Walker's "cultural themes" as they articulated their theological positions. For example, Kelly Brown Douglas, an ordained Episcopal minister teaching at Howard Divinity School in Washington D.C., presents black women as the face of the Black Christ:

> A womanist portrayal of the Black Christ avails itself of a diversity of symbols and icons. These symbols and icons are living symbols and icons as Christ is the living Christ. That is, womanist portrayals of the Black Christ endeavour to lift up those persons, especially black women, who are a part of the black past and present, who have worked to move the black community towards wholeness. These portrayals of Christ suggest, for instance, that Christ can be seen in the face of a Sojourner Truth, a Harriet Tubman, or a Fannie Lou Hamer, as each one struggled to help the entire black community survive and become whole...
>
> Seeing Christ in the faces of those who were and are actively committed to the "wholeness" of the black community suggests... that the Black Christ is present in the black community wherever people are engaged in a struggle for that community's "wholeness"... It challenges black people to participate in activities that advance the unity and freedom of their community... In addition to highlighting the presence of Christ in those who work toward black wholeness, a womanist Black Christ will consistently lift up the presence of Christ in the faces of the poorest black women.[8]

This emphasis on wholeness, survival and commitment to the community's struggle recalls some of the cultural themes Walker articulates and influences the kind of Christology Douglas develops, with more emphasis on Christ in history than on the historical Jesus.

In addition to this cultural influence, political factors and politically influenced theological factors have brought womanist theology to life.

Political factors and political theological factors

The cultural revolutions in the US black community in the 1960s, with their "black is beautiful" motif, gave all black Americans appreciation and pride rather than shame in their blackness. Black Americans searched their African heritage and found a new beauty in African culture — in art, in hair-styles, in fabrics and clothing, in jewelry. This African-American aesthetic, with its emphasis on valuing Africa and blackness, could be used to assess American culture to discover the political use of blackness by the white, dominating culture.

Some womanist analysis showed how the media and other culture-generating sources in the USA had degraded the colour black for centuries, keeping black people outside the economic and political mainstream of American life and implanting in the national psyche the idea of the moral and intellectual inferiority of black people.

Everyday language reinforces the idea of the inferiority of black and the superiority of white: angel food cake is white, devil's food cake dark; *black*mail is illegal; the US economic crash in 1873 was referred to as Black September, the great depression began with a stock market crash on Black Friday, the steep fall in stock prices in 1987 on Black Monday; Protestant congregations continue to sing "Wash me and I shall be whiter than snow", which associates the colour white with purity and perfection; to be *black*listed or *black*balled means to be excluded by others from a job, organization or social group perceived as desirable.[9]

The national consciousness is thus saturated with the idea of black as bad and white as good. So when black Americans publicly proclaimed the "black is beautiful" aesthetic, black people were inspired with a new courage to live their political and religious lives affirming the goodness of blackness and darkness.

Out of the political and cultural affirmation of a black aesthetic, black liberation theology came to life, with its claims of the blackness of God and God's preference for poor black people. This was a stepping-stone for black female theologians on the way to the development of womanist theology. The works of James H. Cone and James Deotis Roberts were especially important for giving black Christians a renewed sense of God's identification with the black struggle for freedom in the late twentieth century. Cone and Roberts used a language honest and powerful enough to express the depth of pain black people had experienced because of racism in North America.

But even as black women affirmed the racial analysis of Cone, Roberts and other black male theologians, they knew there was not "enough material" in black liberation theology to make it fit black women's experience. Black male theologians provided only masculine images of God. Their illustrations of the character of racial oppression in the United States were drawn primarily from male authors and from male experience. Black women's intellectual, cultural, political, aesthetic and social ideas had not been used by black male theologians to construct the ideas in black liberation theology. Womanist theology had to include more than an analysis of white racism.

Similarly, feminist theology was a stepping stone on the way to developing womanist theology. Again, there might not be enough material to make it fit black women, but it proclaimed some mighty truths that black female theologians could not ignore:

— when God is referred to and conceived in exclusively male terms, women are not thought to be in the image of God;
— the Bible has been used in church and society to validate male domination of females;
— the oppression of women is a cross-cultural reality extending to practically every Christian community in the world;
— Christian women need images of the divine that also reflect the female;
— domestic violence and human sexuality are subjects for theological reflection.

Feminist theologians and their works had a profound influence on the theological development of some of the African-American women who ultimately became prominent in the womanist theological movement. Even though their works lack adequate reference to black women's experience, they point out the sexist character of sources important for the development of the Western Christian tradition.

Womanist theology has itself contributed various ideas to the Christian theological enterprise in the areas of biblical hermeneutics, theological doctrine, ethics and a new understanding of the mission of the church.

Some contributions of womanist theology

Womanist Old Testament scholar Renita Weems has begun her biblical scholarship taking cues from the community of black women rather than solely from the academy. She has brought the academy and grassroots black women together as she retells biblical stories from the perspective of these women in a language they can understand. In her book *Just a Sister Away: A Womanist Vision of Women's Relationships in the Bible*, Weems uses her skills as a professionally trained biblical scholar and ordained minister to bridge the gap between church and seminary.

Another womanist New Testament scholar, Clarice Martin, uses a methodology that moves from women's issues in the church to academic scholarship, rather than imposing the world of the academy on the world of women. The exchange between these two worlds is evident in her first published booklet, a study guide on the Acts of the Apostles, produced for women in the Presbyterian Church (USA), *Tongues of Fire: Power for the Church Today*.

Sociologist of religion Cheryl Townsend Gilkes has shown how African-Americans transformed fragments of scripture so that gender equality was achieved:

> Within gospel music, the biblical phrase, "father to the fatherless" (Ps. 68:5) has been linked to such parallel phrases as "mother to the motherless", "brother to the brotherless" and "sister when you're sisterless". This usage points to the special importance of Psalm 68 for black people and extends the image of God to include the feminine and the maternal in worship language.[10]

Gilkes, an ordained Baptist minister and womanist scholar, devotes much scholarly attention to unearthing cultural clues in black history and the black church which help women own and recover their contributions to African-American community life.

Jacquelyn Grant and Kelly Brown Douglas are contributing profoundly to womanist Christology as they develop their notion of Christ as a black woman.[11] A difference between their positions is that Grant sees Christ specifically as a black woman, whereas Douglas postulates a Christ living in the face of black women engaged in working towards the unity and wholeness of the community. Douglas's position is open-ended, in that it leaves space for Christ also to be living in the face of black men engaged in the same activity.

Womanist theologian Annie Ruth Powell is also probing christological questions in relation to black women. As part of the research for a doctoral dissertation, she is interviewing African-American church women to discover what they believe today about God and Jesus.

My own work questions the value given to sacrifice and suffering in the Christian religion. I assert that the way many Christians understand redemption, as gained through the death of an innocent person, is destructive for African-American women, whose oppression includes social-role surrogacy. If we believe Jesus died in the place of sinful humankind, then Jesus — like all surrogates — was filling a role others should have filled. This leads me to an examination of the atonement theories that have been basic to the development of Christian theology.[12]

Anne Elliott, an ordained African Methodist Episcopal minister and Union Theological Seminary doctoral scholar, is exploring the meaning of "the spirit" referred to by African-American women in the churches. She is discovering a black notion of the spirit more related to the doctrines of the Eastern Christian traditions than those of Western Christian traditions. She is also actively working with grassroots black women as the project director of an "alternative to incarceration" programme called Green Hope.

Joy Bostic is designing a womanist theological methodology based on jazz music and the jazz cultural tradition, strands of which thrive in black church music. An ordained Baptist minister, Bostic is also working with Elliott at Green Hope.

Karen Baker-Fletcher's current work assesses the theological import of the life and work of a nineteenth-century black foremother, Annie Julia Cooper. Baker-Fletcher's great contribution to the development of womanist theology is her cultural analysis, which is yielding new insights about the categories best suited for describing the character of African-American women's faith.

Womanists are also making outstanding contributions in ethics. Katie Cannon has done ground-breaking work in her book *Womanist Ethics*, which describes what she calls the "quiet grace" that sustains and inspires the activism of black women and figures greatly in the development of their creative potential.[13]

Womanist ethicist Emilie Townes has edited *A Troublin' in My Soul: Womanist Perspectives on Evil and Suffering*, which contains essays by womanist theologians, biblical scholars, ethicists and ministers on subjects related to evil and suffering. Her own book *Womanist Justice, Womanist Hope* focuses on the contributions to ethics made by reflecting on the biographies of some early black female forebears like Ida Wells Barnet.[14]

Other womanist ethicists are working on projects about black women and inter-structural oppression (Martha Riggs), about black women and the value of difference in the women's movement (Joan Martin) and about black women's experience of nurture and care (Toinette M. Eugene).

By far one of the most significant contributions of womanist theology is the way some of its adherents understand the mission of the church as "The Church Without Walls".[15] Beyond the physical location of church buildings, "The Church Without Walls" comprises a variety of ministries conducted by grassroots lay womanist theologians like Betty Bolden. Bolden, whose theology focuses more on action than on words, is involved in the ministry of community organizing with a group called Harlem Initiatives Together (HIT). One of HIT's basic aims is to develop female and male leadership at the grassroots. Community people identify issues important for improving their own communities, then they devise their own strategic plan to realize the goals associated with these issues.

HIT has helped many African-American ministers to realize that much work is needed in order to organize black communities.

Through HIT and Green Hope womanist theologians, lay and ordained, are steadily expanding The Church Without Walls. This "outside church" preaches no sermons. Rather, the womanist theologians participate in healing and helping poor women (as well as men in HIT) to develop the self-esteem, self-consciousness and self-love they need to sustain their struggle for survival, spiritual renewal and a positive, productive quality of life for themselves and their families.

The development of women's theological voices in the United States has by no means been monolithic. Women in various cultural and racial communities have produced their own ways of talking and writing about women's relation to the divine. The womanist way produced by African-American women is not something to be imposed imperialistically on women from other cultural contexts.

The hope of many womanist theologians is that communities of women from various cultures and countries will develop theologies consistent with their own experiences and cultural heritages. Then women from around the world can come together to share and exchange strategies for women's survival, liberation and leadership in the churches. This kind of exchange will bring the spirit of the kingdom closer to our lives and lead to a more liberated world in which women and men live together in the image of God's freedom and grace.

NOTES

[1] This story is used in Delores S. Williams, "The Color of Feminism: Or Speaking the Black Woman's Tongue", *Journal of Religious Thought*, Vol. 43, spring-summer 1986, pp.42-58.

[2] White feminists, including Letty Russell and Elizabeth Bettenhausen, and black womanists are now working together in an anti-racism programme sponsored by the Women's Theological Center in Boston. Beverly Harrison has developed rigorous anti-racism components in some of her courses at Union Theological Seminary, as has Carter Heyward at Episcopal Divinity School.

[3] Quoted by Elizabeth Hood, "Black Woman, White Woman: Separate Paths to Liberation", *The Black Scholar*, Vol. 4, no. 7, April 1978, p.49.

[4] Jacquelyn Grant, "Black Theology and the Black Woman", in *Black Theology: A Documentary History, 1966-1975*, eds Gayraud S. Wilmore and James H. Cone, Maryknoll NY, Orbis, 1979, p.420.

[5] Delores S. Williams, *Sisters in the Wilderness: The Challenge of Womanist God Talk*, Maryknoll NY, Orbis, 1993.

126   *Women's Visions*

Lee's work first appeared in 1849, Elaw's in 1846. See "The Life and Religious Experience of Jarena Lee" and "Memoirs of the Life, Religious Experience, Ministerial Travels and Labors of Mrs Zilpha Elaw", both in William L. Andrews, ed., *Sisters of the Spirit*, Bloomington, Indiana UP, 1986.

Alice Walker, *In Search of Our Mother's Gardens*, San Diego, Harcourt Brace Jovanovich, 1983, p.xi.

Kelly Brown Douglas, *The Black Christ*, Maryknoll NY, Orbis, 1994, p.108.

For a fuller discussion of the myth of black inferiority, see my *Sisters in the Wilderness*, ch. IV.

Gilkes, "Mother to the Motherless, Father to the Fatherless: Power, Gender and Community in an Afrocentric Biblical Tradition", in *Semeia*, Vol. 47, ed. Elisabeth Schüssler Fiorenza, Atlanta, Scholars Press, 1989.

Jacquelyn Grant, *White Women's Christ and Black Women's Jesus*, Atlanta, Scholars Press, 1989.

Sisters in the Wilderness, pp.161-69, 199f.

Katie Cannon, *Womanist Ethics*, Atlanta, Scholars Press, 1988.

Emilie Townes, ed., *A Troublin' in My Soul*, Maryknoll NY, Orbis, 1993; *Womanist Justice, Womanist Hope*, Atlanta, Scholars Press, 1993.

Betty Bolden, "Church Without Walls", *Voices of Mission*, Fall 1993, published by the National Mission Department of the African Methodist Episcopal Church.

Feminist Theology in Canada

DORCAS GORDON

This paper makes no claim to represent all of Canada, but seeks to provide a window into the work taking place in Canada in feminist analysis. Geographically, I am situated just outside metropolitan Toronto in southwestern Ontario, and my feminist contacts are found primarily in this region. This paper is also limited by my particular social location — that I am English and not French or Native Canadian, that my work is in academia and a congregation and not within a justice or advocacy context.[1]

I teach New Testament studies at Knox College, a seminary of the Presbyterian Church in Canada affiliated to the Toronto School of Theology. Therefore, I am most familiar with feminist questions as they impact biblical hermeneutics. To give some insight into the issues around women found in a specific ministry setting, I will use the example of the Presbyterian Church in Canada, the denomination within which I work as an ordained minister and with whose structures and interests I am most familiar.

Biblical hermeneutics

Within feminist biblical hermeneutics on the Canadian scene a number of different strategies are identifiable. These multiple approaches embrace the whole range presented by biblical scholars such as Elisabeth Schüssler Fiorenza.[2]

Some of our work continues a revisionist or remedial aim: to raise awareness of women's centrality in the story of faith. This research is not only carried out within the canonical writings, but also encourages extra-canonical and cross-cultural research about women in antiquity. For example, Margaret Y. MacDonald of the department of religious studies at the University of Ottawa has used models from the sociology of knowledge to examine the increasing institutionalization of the Pauline churches, focusing on how that affected women and their ministry. Articles on 1 Corinthians 7, which include "Women Holy in Body and Spirit" and "Early Christian Women Married to Unbelievers", not only seek to recover forgotten traditions about women, but also work to remove the centuries-old layers of androcentric interpretation that cover up the supposed original meaning of the biblical text. To recover biblical women from their marginality is an increasingly popular topic for women's workshops at the grassroots level.

Only slowly are courses being offered at the seminary level which specifically introduce questions of feminist interpretation or the nature of the authority of scripture and of the canon. It is difficult to assess how much feminist analysis takes place in the context of other teaching. At the grassroots I perceive such questions to be less welcome, even viewed with suspicion within some contexts. When the Women's Missionary Society in the Presbyterian Church in Canada, a well-organized tradi-tional network of women, adopted the Ecumenical Decade study *We Belong Together: Churches in Solidarity with Women* as one of its study materials in 1993, reaction was mixed. None who responded officially rated the material enthusiastically. Most commented on the diverse opinions within their group on such issues as women's oppression, inclusive language and the like. One group wrote that "some parts of the study are worldly, profane, blasphemous" and called it "an attempt to convince, brainwash women that we need to make a shift in our understanding and interpretation of the Bible". The distressing thing is that this reaction comes from an organization with a strong history of women's ministry, a history of strong women.

Other examples of feminist biblical work are concerned with the androcentric character of biblical texts and discuss their proper transla-tion. In my work in New Testament studies, I teach introductory Greek and am continually reminded — and seek to remind my students — of the power of discourse and language. Specific work is needed on the functioning of grammatical gender and grammatically masculine texts in informing reality and enforcing women's marginality and absence from the story. It is critical for this research to make its way into worship and liturgy. At present within my denomination these questions remain primarily on the margins of thought and expression — viewed as a women's issue, not the church's issue.

The work carried out by Canadian feminist biblical scholars is not culturally distinct from that of our counterparts in the United States.

When I sought to define a Canadian identity in terms of biblical hermeneutics, I more often found publications which included the work of both Canadian and US feminists. For example, a 1989 volume edited by Peggy Day, an Old Testament professor at the University of Winnipeg, included articles on Old Testament women which address gender-nuanced questions using a range of strategies.[3] In keeping with feminist analysis these strategies were informed by theoretical propositions put forward and methodological advances made in disciplines such as sociology, anthropology, literary criticism, history, classics, folklore studies and especially women's studies. Two of the articles in this volume are by Canadian scholars.

Day identifies many of the critical issues in biblical hermeneutics with which we all work. She discusses the ongoing dialectic between tradition and experience and the fact that both text and translation reflect predominantly male experience. A tenet of the book is that only when male experience does not contradict or deny female experience can the text be expected to contain theological truth.

Central to this discussion is the myth of objectivity in biblical interpretation and the corollary demand that all interpreters identify their social location — their particular interest in interpreting a text — and allow scrutiny of their methodology in light of its possibilities and limitations. An important aspect of this critique is the asking of questions that can expose the limitations within interpretative frameworks. Here the cross-cultural emphasis in biblical interpretation provides an example, with its attempt to broaden the interpretative framework of biblical studies in order to expose the limitations of having only one voice reading the text.[4]

Day affirms that the essays in *Gender and Difference*

> offer concrete examples of the kinds of questions that need to be asked when attention is paid to gender. With regard to modern biblical scholarship, they question the value and sometimes the validity of previous studies that have not taken gender into account, document instances wherein gender biases typical of modern, western worldviews have been inappropriately read into the material under study, and implicitly challenge the interpretive frameworks that have characterized and limited the discipline's formulation of questions.[5]

The two articles by Canadian scholars are: "From the Child is Born the Woman: The Story of Jephthah's Daughter" by Day and "Women of the Exodus in Biblical Retelling of the Second Temple Period" by Eileen Schuller, a Qumran scholar teaching at McMaster Divinity School in

Hamilton, Ontario, who has also written the article on the Apocrypha in the *Women's Bible Commentary*.

Systematic theology

Ellen Leonard, a Roman Catholic scholar and feminist theologian, has sought to add to our understanding of the formative place of experience, drawing attention to the need not only to recover present experience in its full social and political dimensions as foundational for theology, but also to correct the bias in the experience which plays a foundational role in theology.[6] The latter she deals with at great length, citing "new theologies" which argue that Western theology is "culture-bound, church-centred, male-dominated, age-dominated, pro-capitalist, anti-communist, non-revolutionary and overly theoretical".[7]

Describing her life as a Canadian woman and feminist, Leonard identifies three experiences which have helped her to rethink her theology, particularly her image of God and her understanding of anthropology, Christology and ecclesiology. These three are transition points within the Canadian experience: from survival in the wilderness to survival in the world; from colonial status to global responsibility; from maintaining French and English culture to the acceptance and affirmation of pluralism. Paralleled by a feminist concern for ecology, empowerment and respect for different voices, these allow her to understand the larger issues through the personal and the particular. In her conclusion she states:

> By listening to the stories of various groups we discover how God is revealing God's self today. The theologian's task is to listen with attention and humility to what God is doing in our complex world. New voices are being raised and these voices need to be heard... It is not enough that the new voices speak to one another.[8]

Quoting David Tracy, she continues:

> All the victims of our discourses and our history have begun to discover their own discourses in ways that our discourse finds difficult to hear, much less to listen to... We have just begun to sense the terror of that otherness. But only by beginning to listen to those other voices may we also begin to hear the otherness within our own discourse and within ourselves. What we then might begin to hear, above our chatter, are possibilities we have never dared to dream.[9]

The need to reclaim the experiences of those not included will continue to be a challenge for theology and biblical interpretation in Canada.

Leonard's work focuses on Christology. In her 1990 presidential address to the Canadian Theological Society, "Women and Christ: Towards Inclusive Christologies",[10] she recognized the struggle for contemporary Christologies of the implications of the claim of universal significance for Christ, especially for the inclusivity of Christology from the perspective of Jewish-Christian dialogue, interfaith dialogue, ecological concerns and women. Her address develops around a number of questions: What is the significance of the maleness of Jesus? Does it support the view of the male as normative humanity? Does it reveal God as male? How has the symbol been used in the praxis of the community? Is it possible to develop a Christology which is non-androcentric, a Christology truly inclusive of women and men? What would Christology be like if it were truly inclusive? And perhaps most important, how might popular devotion image Christ in ways that do not contribute to male domination?

Leonard begins with her own voice concerning images of Christ, then records the voices of other women she has heard (North American, Asian, Latin American, African-American) and names the voices of women she has not heard even within Canada — Francophone women, native women, immigrant women, poor women. She outlines the problems the Christ symbol poses if one takes seriously women's experiences of embodiment, oppression and interrelatedness and presents five alternative approaches to Christology: Women Christ/Christa, Christ as Incarnate Wisdom/Sophia (Elizabeth Johnson), Jesus as prototype (Schüssler Fiorenza), Jesus as iconoclastic prophet (Rosemary Ruether), Christa/ Community (Rita Nakashima Brock). In conclusion, she challenges Canadian theologians to reflect on the basic ingredients of an inclusive Christology: one which affirms female embodiment, rejects victimization based on patterns of dominance and submission and enables women to move from the past into the present and future.

Two feminists writing on women's spirituality exemplify the work carried out in Canada in this area. Cora Twohing-Moengengongo is an Irish-born Canadian who asks whether it is necessary to speak specifically of women's spirituality. Her answer is yes, because women's full humanity has been restricted in the whole social order, as is clearly seen in the feminization of poverty and the reality of violence and abuse against women, and because of Christian teaching and practice, especially its emphasis on self-sacrifice and self-denial. She criticizes theories of human development which are largely formulated by males based on male experience, and she denounces the remnants of dualism which exist as nature/body/women over against culture/spirit/man.[11]

Charlotte Caron is a diaconal minister in the United Church of Canada and professor of pastoral theology at St Andrew's College, Saskatoon, Saskatchewan. In her book *To Make and Make Again: Feminist Ritual Theology*, she asks how religious rituals nurture and challenge feminists in their work for justice and well-being in the world.

Caron begins by quoting Nellie Morton's question in *The Journey is Home*: What if we remove the sexism from God and there is nothing left? In other words, what if religious experience must have a male bias to exist? What if women's experience of the holy can never be validated? Caron hopes that sexism can be removed from God, that the integration of women's experiences of the holy will help to know something more of God than we currently know and that knowing more of the holy will lead us to a sustainable world order in which justice and peace create a *kin*dom of well-being for all humanity and the world.[12]

Five components are interwoven in Caron's method, which she calls feminist theological/thealogical: story-telling; a definition of the issues with a hermeneutics of suspicion; an analysis of how the issue reflects and portrays class, economics, geography, gender, race, men's power and women's power; action, the values to be associated with the action, the alternatives and the strategies; theological/thealogical reflection and theory formulation looking at how we might convey the theory and theological/thealogical meaning in new ways. As she listens to a wide variety of voices and women's stories, new ways of naming the holy emerge in terms such as community, vulnerability, beauty, loss, embodiment, survival and resistance. The interviews that form the heart of her research reveal that women want rituals to relate to their ordinary experiences, rituals that affirm, strengthen and empower them in their social relationships, economic situations and bodily changes.

An article by Marsha Hewitt, professor of social ethics at the Toronto School of Theology, is entitled "Where Speech Has Lost its Power: A Social Ethical Reflection on the Meaning of Surrogate Motherhood".[13] While this addresses the issue of surrogate motherhood, it speaks first of the power of language and naming.

A hurried perusal of other Canadian journals looking for the type of theological reflection being carried out by women shows a recurrence of themes across denominational lines. In the *Conrad Grebel Review*, a Mennonite publication, the 1991-92 edition included the following articles by women: "Women and Poverty: What is the Church's Role?";

"First Steps on the Journey to Dismantling Racism"; "Domestic Violence: A Challenge to Mennonite Faith and Peace Theology"; "Self-Determination: The Road to Justice". In *Compass*, a Jesuit magazine, a random screening of articles by Canadian women revealed the following: "The Struggle of Refugee Women" by Elsa Tesfay Musa; "The Refugee Commandment: An Invitation to be Neighbours" by Mary Jo Leddy; "The Bible's Ambiguous View of Authority" by Janet Somerville; "Christ and the Cosmos: Renewing the Links" by Anne Lonergan.

Feminist theology and the churches

Ecumenical
The Ecumenical Decade Coordinating Group in Toronto is composed of appointed representative and interested participants from a range of Canadian churches and organizations. Its vision statement, affirming the goals of the Decade, reads as follows:

> To empower women to challenge oppressive structures in the global community, their country and their church; to affirm, through shared leadership and decision-making, the contributions of women in churches and communities; to give visibility to women's perspectives and actions in the work and struggle for justice, peace and the integrity of creation; to enable churches to free themselves from racism, sexism and classism and from teachings and practices that discriminate against women; to encourage churches to take actions in solidarity with women.

The group aims to work ecumenically to help churches and church organizations foster the Decade goals in Canada and to implement them within their own structures. This group identifies four hallmarks of its work:

> 1. To create models to enable women and men to work together; to promote dialogue between women and men and to reflect this in a gender-balanced committee.
> 2. To promote new models of shared leadership and decision-making in our churches and society; to model these in our group and to reflect these in a coordinating group that includes minority voices.
> 3. To provide places and resources through which to creatively rethink our theologies and our vision for social justice. These will reflect a national perspective.
> 4. To approach the work from a feminist perspective; that is to say, a belief in equal rights and opportunities for women, an understanding that women are oppressed and exploited by virtue of being women and a belief in

the power of communities to bring about change that will benefit all of creation.

The group publishes a quarterly magazine, *Groundswell.* In December 1993 it sponsored a forum, "Are the churches in solidarity with women?" which gave mixed reviews — more negative than positive — to the Canadian churches' participation in the Decade. Because of the marginalization of the Decade by the majority of Canadian churches, the coordinating group has had meetings with four or five denominations concerning hopes and expectations of the Decade. An attempt has been made to work more closely with the Canadian Council of Churches and a group known as the Women's Inter-Church Council in order better to accomplish the goals of the Decade. Some have asked how much energy should be spent "convincing" the churches, given that it is clearly the women who own the work of the Decade.

This life and energy of women can be seen in gatherings for spiritual nurture and solidarity work. There is a burgeoning of women's liturgical expression, arts, music, dance, story-telling and biblical reinterpretation.

Care in the use of language and images is a central concern of Betty Radford Turcott, who works with the United Church Women's Organization to raise a feminist consciousness concerning issues of biblical interpretation and inclusive language. She has published a collection of hymns which "trace one woman's personal faith journey as she seeks and finds God in the valleys and high places of everyday life and in the witness of our biblical foremothers".[14]

Anglican feminist Mary Kathleen Speegle Schmitt has written *Seasons of the Feminine Divine: Christian Feminist Prayers for the Liturgical Cycle*, a collection seeking to provide an opportunity for people to engage in prayer that values women's life experience in the context of the Judaeo-Christian tradition. Distinguishing between nonsexist, inclusive and emancipatory ways of including women in the male-oriented language of the Judaeo-Christian liturgical tradition, she chooses emancipatory inclusion: to claim terms that have been derogatory and to value what has been devalued in our language. Many of the names used for God are metaphorical images drawn from the female experience, the female body cycle and nature. Some of the female images are drawn directly from the Bible; others are not. Sometimes Jesus Christ is named in the feminine to express the androgynous character of Christ's work as liberating the oppressed and to name the connection between Christ and the feminine Wisdom of the Hebrew tradition.

Images of Ourselves: The Faith and Work of Canadian Women, published by the Ecumenical Decade Coordinating Group, brings together worship resources, meditations and devotional material written by women. In providing an opportunity for women across Canada to reflect on a variety of facets of their faith and experience, the book draws on contributions from women in nine provinces embracing seven denominations.

The Decade Coordinating Group is strongly committed to economic justice issues, and work with the Taskforce on the Feminine Face of Poverty has been one of its priorities. A further project is an economic literacy kit for use by women's groups.

In writing this paper I asked the coordinator of the Decade group what she saw as the major ongoing challenges arising out of the Ecumenical Decade. The first one she identified was violence against women. Most major Canadian denominations have recently developed policy and procedures concerning sexual harassment and sexual abuse. The task now is to make individual congregations and judicatories aware of these and to help people see their urgency. My own work at the congregational level has shown me how reluctant people are to see the need for such a policy and how readily examples of false charges by women are brought forward in order to discount the need for any policy.

The demand for work on the issue of violence and abuse is ongoing. Only slowly are we in Canada waking up to the insecurity of the lives of many women and the tenuous circumstances in which they survive. The murder of fourteen women in Montreal in 1989 by a man who hated feminists left Canadians reeling from shock. The death of individual women at the hands of disaffected spouses and others continues at a frightening rate.

A second issue mentioned by the coordinator was the need for healthier working partnerships between women and men. Conversations are needed to define what this new way of working together might look like and what kind of assumptions and new structures it will demand. The urgency of this need can be seen in the churches' marginalization of the Ecumenical Decade.

An example from one denomination

The Presbyterian Church in Canada is a small middle-of-the-road denomination whose historical roots are in Scotland. While the church is still predominantly Anglo-Saxon in make-up, its congregations in the major cities are more and more ethnically mixed.

The first thing that must be said is that the Decade plays little or no part in most local congregations. The most common reaction when the Decade is mentioned in a congregation is a blank stare. The work being done is carried out at the national and local levels by groups of interested women.

At the national level — whether because of the Ecumenical Decade or the United Nations focus on women — some important and exciting things are happening, many of them ecumenical. When I approached my denomination for information, some of the most forward-looking material I received came from Presbyterian World Service and Development, the church's development agency. The material I received included a draft copy of its gender policy, profiles of four development projects involving and benefiting women, papers on women and AIDS, violence against women, women's human rights, gender issues and refugees.

The challenges facing the denomination's two specifically women's groups — the Women's Missionary Society and the Order of Diaconal Ministries — are enormous. Ewart College, built by women's money and dedicated to women's ministry, has just been sold, at a time when money is desperately needed for every form of theological education. The battle is on to ensure that the proceeds from this sale are used for women's ministry in the 21st century.

One committee within the ministry and church vocations agency focuses on women in professional ministry. There is no women's desk, and one executive assistant gives ten percent of her time to this committee's work. The effectiveness of this committee seems to be limited. Located in Toronto, it has had difficulty networking across the country. In many presbyteries there may only be one or two women ministers of word and sacrament or diaconal ministers, and they are usually separated by great distances. Moreover, many women in the church are suspicious of this Toronto-based group of feminists. A book of sermons by women has been published to celebrate the twenty-fifth anniversary of the denomination's decision to ordain women to ministry of word and sacrament and to eldership.

This information about the Presbyterian Church in Canada is not meant to focus on the strengths and weaknesses of a particular denomination, but rather because I judge it to be fairly typical of what is happening and is not happening in the country.

My own reflection impresses upon me the many issues that will challenge women of vision in the next century. Some exciting research is being carried out in seminaries and universities. At the level of the

Ecumenical Decade Coordinating Group and in some areas within the denominations, consciousness has been and continues to be heightened as to the goals of the Decade. Many women at the grassroots level, however, remain unconnected to the need for change when it concerns the church — its theology, its language, its structures and its assumptions, especially if that change challenges long-held understandings of the authority of the scripture. The word "feminist" continues to have negative associations in the minds of many women. How these women might be empowered to engage in critical theological reflection in their own context is a crucial question.

NOTES

[1] A valuable resource is *Canadian Network Resources for Feminist Theology and Spirituality*, a book of names, addresses, specialities, course offerings and publications of women of various denominations across the country prepared by the Ecumenical Decade Coordinating Group, with whom I have worked in preparing this paper. The women to whom I refer are all included in this publication. For the analysis of trends and issues within systematic theology in Canada, I received input from Pamela Dickey Young, a feminist theologian and dean of women at Queen's University in Kingston, Ontario.

[2] Cf. *But She Said: Feminist Practices of Biblical Interpretation*, Boston, Beacon Press, 1992, pp.21-39. These strategies are: remedial and revisionist, text and translation, imaginative identification, women as authors and biblical interpreters, historical interpretation, socio-cultural reconstruction, ideological inscription, women as subjects of interpretation, socio-political location.

[3] *Gender and Difference in Ancient Israel*, Minneapolis, Fortress, 1989.

[4] This emphasis is exemplified in Elisabeth Schüssler Fiorenza, ed., *Searching the Scriptures: A Feminist Introduction*, New York, Crossroad, 1993, which includes essays by European, Asian, womanist and *mujerista* biblical interpreters. While no Canadians are among the contributors, its aims are very much in keeping with those of Canadian biblical scholars.

[5] *Op. cit.*, p.3.

[6] Ellen Leonard, "Experience as a Source for Theology: A Canadian and Feminist Perspective", *Studies in Religion*, Vol. 19, 1990, pp.143-62.

[7] *Ibid.*, p.146.

[8] *Ibid.*, p.161.

[9] *Ibid.*, pp.161f.

[10] Published in *Toronto Journal of Theology*, Vol. 6, 1990, pp. 266-85.

[11] "Within the Womb of the Earth, Resplendent with Mystery: Women's Spirituality", *Grail*, Vol. 6, 1990, pp.17-33.

[12] *To Make and Make Again*, New York, Crossroad, 1993, p.2.

[13] In *Toronto Journal of Theology*, Vol. 6, 1990, pp.44-55.

[14] *Songs for the Journey*, Toronto, Women's Inter-Church Council of Canada, 1993.

Feminist Homiletics:
Strategies for Empowerment

CAROL J. SCHLUETER

Feminist homiletics arises out of a community of people, a substantial number of them women, discussing the biblical material in the context of their lives. It does not arise from individuals writing sermons in isolation using solitary exegesis. Feminist homiletics recognizes what I call the Canada Goose Principle. Canada geese fly in a "V" formation, and no one bird is always the leader, but each takes its turn. Upon tiring, the leader drops back and another bird replaces it. The well-being of each bird is important to the survival of the flock; and the more birds that share in the leadership, the easier it is for the flock to progress well. Applied to our topic, this principle suggests preparing sermons in collaboration with the ideas and experiences of others in one's context.

The term "homiletics" comes from the Greek *homilein*, "to converse together". It is used in Luke 24:14-15 of the disciples on the road to Emmaus. They were "talking with each other", discussing their lives and the events of the past 72 hours, especially the painful event of the death of Jesus. The text tells us that the risen Christ joined them. This is the gospel we must preach: that in our experiences, even in the midst of tears and pain, the risen Christ is present.

In conversing together we tell stories in order to make sense out of our lives. We say, "on this particular day, this and this happened and then that and that", and then we say what it all means to us. To speak gospel, good news, is to locate God's presence, incarnation, in the story.

To enact gospel is of course the essence of life. It has been said that our lives are the only gospel some people will ever read. Mary John Mananzan has said that "only the one who is involved in women's struggle is permitted to reflect upon feminist theology". I would add that only the one who is involved in women's struggles should be allowed to preach. Perhaps then biblical texts would no longer be used to justify the abuse of and violence against women. Too many young women from Christian homes tell of being sexually abused by fathers who used quotations from the Bible to defend their right to do so. Families are sometimes said to know about sexual abuse yet do nothing about it, believing that a father as head of the household has a right to control the members of his family.[1] Many women stay in abusive situations and bury their spirits, reluctant to dismantle the two main foundations of their identity — family and religious community. Perhaps if all who preach were to listen to women who have been abused, hold their bruised bodies and walk with them as they look for work and try to rebuild life, no woman would ever again hear a minister or priest admonish her to "go home and try to be a better wife" or "keep the family together for the sake of the children". When abused women's bodies are the hermeneutic we use to read scripture, then our sermons and our lives will be passionate about social, political and ecclesial change.

In this paper I will discuss two strategies for feminist biblical homiletics: feminist narrative imagination and feminist artistic representation.

Feminist narrative imagination

I have said that homiletics has to do with conversing and that conversing is about telling stories. How can stories, specifically New Testament stories, provide new possibilities for women? Let me begin by recalling an event which had a lasting impact on me.

At an engineering school in Montreal, Quebec, fourteen women were murdered in December 1989. A man carrying a gun walked into the school, separated the men from the women, told the men to leave and then, calling the women "feminist bitches", systematically shot and killed them. What happened to those fourteen women could have happened to anyone working to change a social order which gives men the world over privilege and contributes to attitudes that most men acquire: that they have the right to make decisions without consulting more than half the world's population, that their positions give them inherent wisdom, that they may take ever more of the world's resources and that they may control women and children. Too often ecclesiology supports such attitudes. Many of those who are seeking more abundant life for women will be seen by some in society as a threat which needs to be silenced. They will endure insults and intimidating behaviours.

Every time a woman is abused or intimidated in order to silence her, Christ is crucified afresh. This point is graphically made by a controversial bronze sculpture which stands in the garden of Emmanuel College in Toronto. It is called "The Crucified Woman" by Almuth Lutkenhaus. The artist said "she wanted to portray human suffering and, since she was a woman, chose a female body".[2] The slaying of the fourteen women in Montreal was an experience of seeing Christ crucified afresh in the bodies of these young women. How is one to go on after such an event?

This was the same question the two disciples had on their minds as they walked to Emmaus. One of their strategies was storytelling. (The other was given to them: the visual representation of Jesus breaking the bread. We will turn to the discussion of visual representation in the second part of this paper.) To put the process succinctly, the two disciples told the narrative from their perspective and they found Christ present. I call this the use of narrative imagination.

Women's narrative imagination with a biblical text creates a world-view where we might find shelter, celebrate who we are and be transformed for our struggle for a more equitable world, a world which honours the interdependence of nature and all human beings. The attempt here is not so much to be historical as to find meaning from reading the text.

I assume that meaning is made by the reader and in the interaction between the text, the reader and the reader's life experience. I also assume that narrative imagination takes place in a community of people. The responsibility for understanding is "equally shared by author and reader, speaker and listener. It insists on a hermeneutical process that is reciprocal."[3]

The gospel itself, the good news, arises from the experience of God's breaking the bonds of death and raising Jesus to a new life. The gospel accounts are narratives about this experience, and each gospel writer tells the story in a new way for a specific context. Each telling is and is not the reality about which one is trying to speak. In this sense the narrative accounts are metaphorical: for God is both revealed and hidden.[4]

Not only is the reality we are attempting to describe both hidden and revealed, but also the lives of women, even when they are mentioned in the text, are hidden. As the stories stand, they both fit and do not fit reality as we experience it. To take one example, at which we shall look more closely below, we will need to ask questions like, What is the story as told by the woman with the flow of blood? Whose interests are served in the text as it stands? What difference does it make if we focus on the woman herself?

Women must engage in the reciprocal process of text and reader by bringing their experience to bear on the text and by overlapping contemporary women's lives with the text. The story as metaphor has many "loose ends, free spaces for the listener's imagination"[5] and for being retold in a different way.

Feminist narrative imagination is intentional about telling stories which are sacred stories. It is feminist in that it takes seriously women's perspective and experience. It is sacred in that it ignites a process which energizes us to be actively engaged in the struggle for an equitable and ecologically balanced world.

Elizabeth Say has described the biblical narratives as "masculine autobiography" because they are androcentric.[6] If it is true that people make meaning out of their lives through story and that the New Testament narratives as we have them are androcentric, then it is imperative that women remember, reclaim and retell the narratives about women in the New Testament in such a way as to "create their own narrative history"[7] and to structure reality for women's fuller life in the present.

It has been said that "story is a place of possibility".[8] Then let us tell our New Testament narratives as *women's* autobiography, so that they provide more possibilities for women. The telling of New Testament stories has always been a way for people to nurture themselves and gain empowerment. As such, women have always been selective with the biblical text. Renita Weems recalls the story of the grandmother of the noted African-American preacher Howard Thurman, who would not let anyone read Paul's epistles to her because they went against the grain of her sense of human dignity.[9] Her hermeneutic was to accept as scripture only those texts which nurtured her in her goal towards more abundant life and to reject those which did not affirm her personhood. Mary Slessor, a Presbyterian missionary who worked in Africa earlier this century, wrote in her Bible next to the passage in Ephesians 5 which speaks of women being "subject to" their husbands, "Na! Na! Paul, laddie! This will na do!"[10] She, too, read the Bible to reach for more life. In this passage, women's lives served as her hermeneutic. They need to be ours as well. Our hermeneutic must be the aim to have the Bible disclose a world in which women are empowered to walk in the image of God. This goal is faithful to the purpose of the scriptural texts themselves, texts which call for the transformation of people's lives.

When I was seven years old, I received a Bible with pictures from my mother. I especially loved the story of the young slave girl who told Naaman how he could be cured of the leprosy from which he suffered

(2 Kings 5:1-14). I had not read that story in years, and when I reread it recently, I noted with dismay that the slave girl is not named, that she had been a prize of war, separated from her parents and her people, and that it was not she but Elisha who had the wisdom to tell the commander to bathe in the river Jordan. As a little girl, however, I was energized by this story because the heroine was a wise little girl to whom God responded. During my childhood, she was a companion to me. Her life as moral agent helped me to shape my reality and to know who I was.

Then she was a companion of support; today she is a companion of challenge. When I read this story now, I overlap the wise little girl with all the female children of the wars in Rwanda and Bosnia Herzegovina and elsewhere who have been prizes of war, and I shudder. I also shudder when I overlap her with all the female children of the First Nations people in Canada who decades ago were taken from their parents and placed in Christian boarding schools by misguided missionaries. In both cases, I ask what is required of me so that there is more life for these wise little girls and their brothers. There are many unanswered questions and places of silence.

The women in the New Testament can be companions to us in our daily lives if we bring them into the conversation and allow them to tell their stories. I offer some examples.

The woman who puts yeast into measures of flour *(Matthew 13:33/Luke 13:20)*

My life is haunted by the shadow of pollution which threatens our world. If I forget to wear my sunscreen I worry about going outside. A friend of mine has been treated for skin cancer, and a local farmer tells me that the fish in his creek have died because of the fertilizers which have leached out of the fields and into the water. Cattle which graze in the field beside the creek miscarry or give birth to deformed calves. The frogs are disappearing and many trees are dying. A worldview of progress at any price has brought us to the brink of global destruction. These days I buy bottled water.

Into my despair at this situation comes the woman who placed yeast into measures of flour and the whole loaf was filled. This woman has planted the wheat, harvested it and is now making it into something which will nourish many people. I imagine spending time with her and pondering what wisdom she has to teach me. She shows me how she lovingly measures out what she needs and works with it so that it will produce a good bread. This biblical companion, an image of God, tells me how important it is to work with the flour and the yeast and to honour each part as unique and as a gift from God. She teaches me that the wheat, water and yeast have as much right to be here on this earth as do human beings. These things also belong to the earth and they give themselves for our sustanance. We need to honour them and to learn from them. The realm of God is like them: each element is beautiful in itself and exists in relation to others. The three measures of flour are an astounding amount, according to commentators, and would make a great deal of bread. This is what the realm of God is like. It nourishes all.

The woman with the flow of blood
(Matthew 9:18-26/Mark 5:25-34/Luke 8:40-56)
      Many women, even women with successful careers, are plagued with the shadow of self-doubt. They sometimes act out dependency and helplessness in order to bolster others and ensure ongoing closeness with them. Many women fear that their own growth will lead to the disruption or dissolution of close relationships.[11] As I ponder this surprising fact the woman who was healed of a flow of blood sits down beside me. She tells me that she knows all about self-doubt. She was ill for a long while but did not trust her own judgment as to how to receive healing. After twelve years of consulting others, one day she became exasperated with the doctors, each of whom seemed to have a different solution. She had gone along with their suggestions until she had spent all her money. Now she was alone with her need. This was new and frightening for her. Instead of running off to someone else, she began to trust herself. Her inner voice grew stronger and stronger until she knew what to do. She approached Jesus, but this time she did not focus on consulting before acting. She needed to reach out, to act, and she knew that she would be healed if she did. She was determined to touch Jesus. She simply reached out and touched him. And then, the text says, "she knew within herself that she had been healed". This biblical companion knew how to trust herself. By overlapping their lives with hers, contemporary women can learn from her courage and her ability to risk.
      One of my students, Paula Wansbrough, has connected this biblical story to some traditions about St Veronica from the *Acts of Pilate*, a gnostic interpretation in Irenaeus' *Against the Heresies* and an ancient play called *Corpus Christi*. These accounts of the woman with the flow of blood (sometimes called Bernice and at other times Veronica) reveal a woman who defends Jesus at his trial, speaks out against a hostile crowd, wipes his weary face with her veil on his way to Calvary, is astonished by

the image of his face appearing on the veil, assists in the conversion of the emperor by producing the veil with its image and is an agent of healing by using the veil. In making connections with the lives of modern women who are often focussed on others,[12] Paula presented a woman who knew about self-care not only in taking steps to gain healing for herself but also in having the courage to defend her convictions. In speaking out for Jesus in the presence of a hostile crowd she subverts the dominant social structure by breaking the social codes for women's behaviour. She gives voice to her impulse for justice. She participates in a reciprocal relationship of care-giving with a man. She is a preacher and an apostle through voice and actions; and she arouses us to rethink God — an incarnate God who values small acts of mercy, showing us God's approachability. We can easily observe the richness of this story for constructing a narrative history in which modern women are nourished.

The Syro-Phoenician woman
(Matthew 15:21-28/Mark 7:24-30)
    One summer, while in a small town in northern Ontario, I discovered a Native People's reserve nearby. When I drove through it, the poverty and unemployment were obvious. I saw a trailer at one end of the reserve. There was a sign on it — "Jesus Saves" or something like that — and the name of a minister, a woman. I was curious. I wondered what she was doing on this reserve. She was not at home, but her neighbour was. When she came to the door of her home, I was surprised to see that she had bleached blonde hair. I wondered whether the predominantly white culture in Canada had led her to devalue her own beautiful black hair and dark skin? Had she chosen the colour freely or was she doing it to fit into the prevailing culture? I was troubled by my own heritage and the imperialism by which it has gained a better life at the expense of those First Nations to whom Canada belonged.
    As I mull this over, a woman from Mark's gospel comes and sits beside me. She knows what it is to be considered a second-class citizen, but with a twinkle in her eye she tells me how one day she challenged the prevailing culture in the person of Jesus and won. Such victories are few, and I eagerly lean forward to hear her story. Her daughter had been ill and she had asked Jesus to heal her. He had responded that he had been called only to the house of Israel, that it was not right to take the children's bread and to throw it to the dogs. She suddenly felt smaller and ashamed. While her ego smarted at that insult, she thought of her daughter and quickly responded, "Yes, Lord, but even the dogs under the table eat the crumbs

which fall from the children's table." She saw him look startled, then his eyes met hers and he saw her for the first time as his equal. He said, "You are right. Perhaps there is room for all at the table. Your daughter is well."

This woman challenges me really to see the people on that Native People's reserve, to see them as equal partners at the table of opportunity and resources, to listen to what they have to say and to share my bread. This woman companion walks with me and points out those people whom I sometimes do not acknowledge. Our companionship is transformative.

Mary and Elizabeth
(Luke 1:39-56)

There are many other companions for us to find in the stories of the New Testament. The story of Mary and Elizabeth tells of a very young woman who is pregnant going to visit her older cousin Elizabeth, who is also pregnant. Most commentaries focus on the relation of the unborn John the Baptist and the unborn Jesus. More recent commentaries point to the importance of Mary's song, which announces the kind of kingdom which God is initiating.[13] This song is a beautiful witness to Mary as a proclaimer of God's new ways. She is a prophetess and a disciple.

But the part I enjoy so much comes in verse 56: "And Mary stayed with her for about three months and then returned to her home." Three months! One can imagine the conversations, the support for each other, the wisdom learned from each other. This is a powerful verse about women's support, mentoring and wisdom — realities we want to affirm. It is essential for us to reclaim this verse.

The raising of Lazarus
(John 11:1-46)

Feminist narrative imagination is easiest when we work with a story about women, but there are strategies like role reversal which we can use with other stories to have them overlap with women's lives. For example, we might experiment with what difference a story of the raising of a female Lazarus would make.

Michel Manson has created a visual representation of a female Lazarus. She has painted the lower part of her body wrapped in bands of grave cloth. The bands are coming undone and the ends of them are unwinding and becoming colourful ribbons. Her face and hands are gaining colour and life as she raises them in praise and thankfulness, but there is a small tear in the corner of her eye. Manson has shown us that with freedom comes pain. This visual piece provides hope for all who work for the liberation of women and who await the celebration of their gifts to the church and world.

What would it mean for modern women to identify with a female Lazarus who was bound and dead and to have Jesus call her forth to life again? What would it mean for women of the North and the South to speak together of their stories of being bound and dead for days? In what ways are we dead? What would it mean for us to weep for each other in order to call each other forth from death to life? What ritual could we construct to acknowledge our different experiences, allow us really to hear one another (especially when some of us are complicit in causing another's pain), affirm our connectedness and empower us all to work towards life?

Lydia
(Acts 16:15)
    Where the biblical story is silent, we need to write about those parts. What was Lydia thinking as she, a new convert and a Gentile, invited Paul and his companions to her house? Was she worried that she would not be accepted? Did she give up? The story says, "She prevailed upon them...". This story has a great deal of potential for dealing with the topics of racism and sexism and how women can act against them on the basis of life in Christ.

    We have seen, then, that biblical stories and contemporary women's lives can overlap in ways that are affirming and empowering to women, that challenge them and that can transform them. Such work with feminist narrative imagination can ignite a process which leads to a sense of one's place in God's story, a sense of its being "my story".

Feminist artistic representations

    The earliest church knew the power of the symbol, the visual. The symbol of the fish spoke volumes of hope to people's lives. In the story of the disciples walking to Emmaus, the breaking of the bread was the strong visual representation which told them in metaphorical fashion that God had broken death and real life had emerged.

    The impact of the visual on our social and spiritual lives should not be underestimated. Newspapers and television bombard us with images of how life is to be lived. In an age when television has become a substitute storyteller,[14] we learn stories which tell us that women's menstrual flow is a problem rather than a natural cleansing process, that women need to protect themselves from the natural process of ageing and that women are naturally stupid and need to be educated about such matters as which laundry detergent to use — sexist stereotypes which persist despite twenty years of efforts to eradicate them. Further, women too often receive images that communicate that they are vulnerable victims, which can only lead to fear and loss of self-esteem. We need strong visual images to compensate for the daily imprinting of such images, images which portray women as agents of their own growth, agents of change in social roles, agents of change towards a more just society for all and essential contributors to all theological discussions.

Traditional visual representations of biblical women often had them in seated positions and displaying dependent gestures. Some artists — like Michel Manson with her "Female Lazarus" — are effectively overlapping the struggle of modern women for more life with the biblical stories. Representing the process of transformation from death to life, the Female Lazarus is a resource for empowerment.

Similarly, Elizabeth Frick's sculpture at Salisbury Cathedral in England of a middle-aged Mary striding out towards the world brings a new dimension to the notions of women's lives. She is not defined by either children or husband. While she may relate to both, she is complete in herself. Furthermore, she is on the move, giving her energy to those projects which she chooses. As a model for contemporary women and a thought piece for the biblical figure of Mary, she expands the possibilities for living as a self-confident, active, strong middle-aged woman.

Art proposes a world for our consideration as a source for a new way of living. It is a window into a self-contained world and a mirror in which we can see ourselves. "Art is a type of story. Art, as a prophetic reflection on the context in which we live, is an agent of transformation."[15] As agents of transformation, artistic pieces overlap our stories and are different from them.

We need to learn to be art users, that is, to use images for self-reflection. An art user allows images to address her and surrounds herself with images which affirm her, tranform her and challenge her to change culture. If artistic expressions of the diverse life experiences and capabilities of women could imprint us as much as those which deplete women of their creative energy, we would bring to our lives more *energeia* (the Greek word for a "working power") and see ourselves more consistently as the strong, creative women that we are. I offer some other examples.

The Lenten Cloth

The Lenten Cloth by Lucy de Sousa from India is an artistic piece which reveals a new world. Entitled "The Growing of the Kingdom of God", this cloth of seven frames depicts women in a mandala-like structure, beginning with the central frame which depicts the woman who put yeast into three measures of flour and then continuing out in a circle to show Miriam and her sisters dancing after their liberation from slavery; the midwives Shiprah and Puah saving baby boys from the rage of the Pharaoh; Ruth, Naomi and Boaz talking in a field of grain; Mary and Elizabeth greeting one another; the Canaanite woman asking Jesus to heal her daughter; and Mary Magdalene proclaiming the good news of Jesus' resurrection to the disciples hiding behind the door of an inner room.

With deep, vibrant, warm colours, this cloth recalls some of the women of our faith history and shows them as central to the stories. The cloth provides a window into women's history and a mirror for us to see the world in a new way. We look at the frames of strong ordinary women who choose life and pull it from the grip of those who would snuff it out. In these frames we do not see women as victims. We see a world of women who are bright and capable and resourceful.

"She, at Home"

Stained glass windows often portray role models of discipleship for worshippers. Many portray St Paul or one of the four evangelists. Even though many women, like the courageous and self-confident Hemorhissa, were remembered in the catacombs in Rome up to the third century, they are seldom commemorated in stained glass any longer. If they were, what would be their impact on us? Would we experience them as transformative?

Recently I saw an artistic expression in stained glass honouring the activities of women like my own grandmother. The image of this work has stayed with me, and I wish that my grandmother could see it. "She, At Home", created by Deborah J. Fleming, depicts a spinning wheel, some canned goods, some freshly cleaned clothes pinned to a washline and some flowers.

My grandmother was an enormously creative and resourceful woman. During the great depression in Canada during the 1930s she laboured night and day. In addition to keeping several large gardens and butchering the meat on a self-sufficient farm, she made soap, worked coats into skirts for her daughters and shirts for her sons, bought the wool of one sheep in the spring and then cleaned it and spun it and knitted stockings and mittens.

In her art, Fleming has enshrined with dignity the work of many of our grandmothers. By her work and in our appreciation of it, their lives are not forgotten and their creativity is valued. The link between us is made stronger. We are called to be creative today, perhaps in a different way, but the creative threads continue.

Many artistic works and illustrations of New Testament stories do not acknowledge the role of women in the life of Jesus. Women need to create artistic pieces and illustrations which set the record straight and open up new possibilities for women's empowerment. We also need to ensure that children's Sunday School material reflects the presence and contribution of women in the early Christian movement, so that the women of the future can walk strong in the biblical story which is theirs.

Creating new patterns

Interweaving our stories with the biblical stories, whether through feminist narrative imagination or feminist artistic representation, is like weaving. Any weaver knows that setting up a loom involves hours of work and the use of many threads. When the loom is completely threaded, the weaving can begin. In the process of the work, each change of gear by the weaver results in two changes. At intervals, it brings forward some threads, letting others recede to the background, and it creates new patterns.

Similarly, our work with narrative and art pulls forward some threads while others recede for a time in the effort to create new patterns which can lead us in ways that celebrate our presence and contributions.

There are of course many tangles which keep the full pattern of women's creativity from surfacing. Many women's voices are not yet heard. The writing of far too few women is available in print, and far too much of what is in print comes from white middle-class women or women educated in the Western world. There is a fear of feminism and a reluctance to read women's work. The church still blocks women's full creativity in myriad ways. Last but not least, there is the great danger that feminist Christians might become anti-semitic by comparing first-century material about an itinerant preacher with Jewish legal material from the second, fourth and sixth centuries. As Judith Plaskow has shown, the largely unconscious motive is to preserve the image of Jesus the liberator of women over against a negative view of Judaism, all the while ignoring both the literature which presents Jewish men as having positive behaviour and attitudes towards women and the passages in the New Testament which are ambivalent towards women.[16]

I do not propose that narrative imagination and working with artistic expression will untangle all of this. However, if the use of feminist narrative or artistic representations ignites a process of *energeia*, so that we experience new visions of women as moral agents, then perhaps the tangles can be attended to lovingly and respectfully, rather than being torn out, cut off or ignored.

In the process of untangling, many stories will be told. If they are sacred stories, then they will ignite *energeia* for the further work of more social equity, more honour for cultural and religious diversity and more commitment to maintain a precious ecological balance.

Mostly it will be hard, thankless, wearying, hopeless and often death-making work, but I pray that in the midst of it all as we "converse together" *(homilein)*, tell each other our stories of pain, we will recognize the risen Christ among us who listens to us, talks with us, stays with us and makes present to us in a concrete visual way God's death-breaking and life-affirming presence. Then our hearts will burn within us. The disciples on the road to Emmaus went on their way with renewed energy and a new way of seeing life. May that always happen to us.

NOTES

[1] Carolyn Holderread Heggin, *Sexual Abuse in Christian Homes and Churches*, Scottdale PA, Herald Press, 1993.

[2] Doris Jean Dyke, "Crucified Woman: Art and the Experience of Faith", *Toronto Journal of Theology*, Vol. 5, 1989, p.163.

[3] Belden C. Lane, "Language, Metaphor, and Pastoral Theology", *Theology Today*, Vol. 43, 1987, pp.489-90; see also Wolfgang Iser, "Indeterminacy and the Reader's Response in Prose Fiction", in *Aspects of Narrative*, ed. J. Hillis Miller, New York, Columbia UP, 1971, p.43.

[4] Cf. Sallie McFague, *Metaphorical Theology: Models of God in Religious Language*, Philadelphia, Fortress, 1982, p.134: "The narrative structure of reality, when viewed through the eyes of religious faith, is always fundamentally metaphorical. It is a way of talking about the events of history and of present experience that acknowledges that what one says about events and their meaning both is and is not true to the reality about which one is attempting to speak. It both is and is not true to the facticity of those events. And it both is and is not true to the meaning of the activity of God, for God both is revealed and remains hidden. That is the meaning of metaphor. It always partakes of the *is* and the *is not*." See also Lane, *loc. cit.*, p.490.

[5] Lane, *ibid.*, p.489.

6 Elizabeth A. Say, *Evidence on Her Own Behalf: Women's Narrative as Theological Voice*, Savage, MD, Rowman & Littlefield, 1990, p.111.

7 *Ibid.*

8 Richard Lewis, "The Story the Child Keeps", in *Sacred Stories*, eds Simpkinson and Simpkinson, p.142.

9 Renita Weems, "Reading Her Way Through the Struggle: African American Women and the Bible", in *Stony the Road We Trod, African American Biblical Interpretation*, ed. Cain Hope Felder, Minneapolis, Fortress, 1991, pp.57-77.

10 James Buchan, *The Expendable Mary Slessor*, Edinburgh, St Andrews, 1980, p.195.

11 Cf. Harriet Goldhor Lerner, "Work and Success Inhibitions", in *Women in Therapy*, New York, Harper & Row, 1988, pp.171-199: "Female anxiety and guilt about ambitious strivings and the exercise of competence are so ubiquitous that the 'fear of success' syndrome has become a household word. Women do indeed fear that they will pay dearly for their accomplishments. They frequently equate success, or the very wish for it, with loss — loss of femininity and attractiveness, loss of significant relationships, loss of health, or even loss of life."

12 See Carol P. Christ, *Diving Deep and Surfacing: Women Writers on Spiritual Quest*, Boston, Beacon Press, 1980, p.19: "In this culture women are encouraged to be receptive to the needs of others — to please or nurture parents, children, spouses, lovers..." Christ notes that this orientation encourages women in "sin through self-negation".

13 Carol A. Newsom and Sharon H. Ringe, *The Women's Bible Commentary*, London, SPCK, 1992, pp.284-85.

14 Richard Lewis, *loc. cit.*, p.137.

15 Cf. Dyke, *loc. cit.*; Susanne Langer, "The Cultural Importance of Art", in *Philosophical Sketches*, New York, Mentor, 1962, p.79.

16 See Judith Plaskow, "Blaming Jews for Inventing Patriarchy", *Lilith*, Vol. 7, 1980, pp.11-12.

Feminist Ecclesiology: An Orthodox Perspective from Australia

LEONIE B. LIVERIS

One of the pleasures of researching women's history, particularly in the church, is the delight of stumbling across women of the past who remind us that we are part of a long journey in which women are claiming and reclaiming their place in the church. We are laying foundations and recovering the truths of women in order to complete an *ecclesia* in which we will fully participate and be embraced in all our diversity and uniqueness.

My comments in this paper reflect my own context and experiences within the Greek Orthodox Church in Australia, a minority migrant church still unable to relinquish past memories and "homeland" culture and to put down roots in Australia's psyche and history. I do not speak of other jurisdictions or other places.

The hesitancy of Orthodox women to be involved in feminist theological scholarship is well known to many Christian feminists. Unlike past centuries, this century has produced too few women's voices in our church questioning church teaching, the prevalent anti-woman rhetoric of the fathers and the theologians and the negative, demeaning and woman-denying practices in church Tradition and tradition. Some of the women who did so in the past now wear the holy crowns of martyrdom, but the few voices of this kind today are ignored or publicly criticized and even dismissed as heretical. I shall try in this paper to set a few small building blocks on emerging foundations, which may provide some hope for the few women and their daughters who are seeking inclusivity and changed structures for community in a church which constantly speaks of its faithfulness as the one true church.

As an historian with a passion for the study of the history of women in the church, particularly their too often reluctantly acknowledged contribution to the Orthodox Church over the centuries, I have been stimulated by Catholic and Protestant feminist theologians and historians who are raising questions about the past which can be applied to us all. Their scholarship offers prophetic, exciting and disturbing theses about the positive presence of women in scripture and church history which challenge present-day hierarchs and conservative theologians. By finding ourselves in scripture and in the early church, we can find ourselves at every other time.

The authority of the church

The Orthodox Church is a scriptural church. The Bible, the supreme expression of God's revelation to humankind, lives and is understood within the church, not over against it; and it is from the church that the Bible ultimately derives its authority.[1]

While the church claims that it alone can interpret Holy Scripture with authority, critical and historical study is not forbidden, though it has not been given the same emphasis as among Protestants or even Catholics; and there is certainly nothing within the Orthodox Church like the biblical hermeneutics now being undertaken by feminist theologians. The Orthodox approach to the faith is fundamentally a liturgical one, that is, through the participation in worship within a church structure. The church is the Body of Christ, the treasury of revealed truths, holy and free of error. So what does this say to women who through culture and tradition are often alienated from full participation in the liturgical life of the church? Remember that for the Orthodox there is no change in liturgical services.

Orthodox women scholars are scattered across the globe. If they publish at all, their work is rarely acknowledged or known beyond their own century, even by more enlightened theologians and historians. For the Orthodox, "the distinctive characteristic of the church is its change-lessness in its loyalty to the past, and its sense of living continuity with the church of ancient times... We do not change the everlasting bound-aries which the fathers have set... but we keep the Tradition just as we received it."[2] This Holy Tradition is made up of Scripture, the councils, the fathers, liturgy, canons and icons. It is little wonder that it is only in the last decade or so that a few women have challenged the traditional place and participation of women in the Orthodox church, even using the words "feminist theology".

Raising questions about centuries of doctrine and dogma which have excluded women from participating in the church equally with men is beyond the strength or spirit of most women. Nor are modern biblical exegesis, historical scholarship and new ways of thinking and writing theology considered as signs of prophetic voices. Like invisible bands of iron across the mind, culture and tradition hold all that has ever been in static, solid blocks of patriarchal rules and expectations. The greatest threat to the few voices challenging the past and the present is the seduction of a few crumbs of praise or approval, for if you are not in, you are out, and that can mean complete isolation. Without an Orthodox feminist network for support, one is isolated not only from church and liturgical life, but often from family and friends, and perceived as a threat to the past two millennia of the true faith.

The history of the Orthodox Church is also a history of the home-church, "which provided equal opportunities for women because traditionally the house was considered women's proper sphere, and women were not excluded from activities in it",[3] and of the church of martyrs, which finally emerged in the fourth century with the "structure and policies of a church based on the ethos of the Roman Empire".[4] Within this ethos the church developed a hierarchical organization and defined all the fundamental doctrines.

A 19th-century woman wrote in an article on "Womanhood and Religious Mis-Education" that "the true spirit of Christianity was issued its death warrant with the decrees of Constantine, the anti-woman statements of the early Fathers and the various councils from which woman was excluded, which met only to wrangle over points of doctrine."[5] And in whatever form we now proclaim ourselves, that process of gradual exclusion is a common tradition for all of us.

A legacy of faithfulness

However, within that common tradition we can also look together at the deeds and words of women of the Bible. We honour their presence on our calendars; we speak admiringly of their work and discipleship, their missionary travels and their martyrdoms. These women, known and unknown, have bequeathed to the church of the late twentieth century their legacy of faithfulness. Feminist theological scholarship throughout the church universal encourages us to broaden our understanding of the women who have given their lives and their questions during the two millennia of the history of the church. Regardless of tradition, they are raising valid questions, building on the work of those early women in a manner appropriate for these times.

If we reflect as women on the life and purpose of Christ during the three brief years of his ministry, we know that he walked among ordinary people, who became his apostles and disciples: the poor, like the widow and her tiny gift to the temple (Mark 12:41-44), the unclean, such as the lepers and the woman who flowed with blood, the despised, including the Samaritan woman at the well, known in the Orthodox tradition as St Photeine, "the enlightened one", the first evangelist who recognized and discussed theology with the Messiah and ran to spread the word among her people (John 4:7-28). The Orthodox Church celebrates St Photeine on 26 February with the hymn

> Illuminated by the Holy Spirit, All-Glorious One, from Christ the Saviour you drank the water of salvation. With open hand you give it to those who thirst, great martyr Photeine, equal to the apostles, pray to Christ for the salvation of our souls.[6]

We use these positive and identifiable examples from Scripture to raise a feminist awareness in the contemporary church. We cannot help observing the close presence of women in all aspects of the ministry of Jesus. Our reflections begin with his birth in humble surroundings, of a courageous and God-centred Jewish young woman, who triumphantly obeyed God's request to bring to life his son. We remember Anna, the aged prophet in the temple, who waited with fasting and prayer, recognized the Christ and praised him mightily (Luke 2:36-38), though she is often lost in the shadow of Simeon. Women not only gave their love, hospitality and unquestioning faith to Christ, but also were steadfast at the cross and the first to proclaim his resurrection. Yet the church today has considerable difficulty acknowledging contemporary women who wish to offer the same ministries within the tradition and practices of the Orthodox Church. Certainly women may offer hospitality, especially when it renders us silent before those receiving our gifts. Silence is indeed seen as a virtue of woman and humility a sign of her grace.

The women who continued their ministry alongside the apostles and other believers in the early church also suffered martyrdom and were apostles and evangelists. The first centuries of the church are filled not only with the history of the early fathers, great monastics and theologians, but also with graphic stories of martyred women, women monastics and saints and great women rulers. Their commitment was continually strengthened and renewed by faith, and their stories and witness are a source of constant admiration and challenge by revealing evidence of women's participatory role in the "royal priesthood of believers" (1 Pet. 2:9). In this time of searching for fuller and more equal participation in our churches, we can do no better than look to the women of our past, particularly those who have been relegated to anonymity or remembered more for their sins than their sanctity.

The denial and exclusion of women today from the inclusive pastoral and preaching roles they assumed in the early church has become a focus of critical exploration by contemporary feminist scholars. For Eva Topping, a Greek Orthodox writer in the USA, the "exclusion of women is based on custom, convention and tradition created by the pride, fears and prejudices of fallible human beings".[7] It is our task to reclaim the inclusive roles and proclaim them for the wholeness of the church; otherwise, "Orthodox women will never enjoy full dignity and equal participation in Orthodoxy's sacramental and liturgical life".[8]

However, there must also be a realism in what we seek. We are not women of the early church, although we absorb their history into our traditions. We are part of a global family, not only a local community. Women today share bitter memories of our cruelty and oppression towards each other. We live in complex societies, within communities that are violent to each other in the name of religion. We struggle each day to maintain civility and extend compassion and love towards those who seem a threat to what we hold precious in our own lives.

Challenging the church

To yearn for a return to the model of the early church is an impossible dream; moreover, the church manifested hierarchical problems in gender relationships very early on. However, we can hope to emulate the qualities of Christian community of which we read in the early church.

We have looked for ways to free ourselves from the oppression of complicated structures weighed down with male theology, male hierarchy and patriarchal laws that leave little space to breathe the freshness of the gospel message. Some women have left the structured church, either relinquishing all faith in Christ and his church or seeking to join or establish communities working for social justice in which the gospel can be lived out. Many others lack the strength or knowledge to challenge the church. All they know is that the church has failed them, and what it offers bears little resemblance to what they seek.

For the Orthodox, leaving the church is seldom an option, for life at home continues as "the little church". The cultural and traditional life and expectations of an Orthodox woman are well entrenched during her upbringing. The home is her power base. An Orthodox, no matter where, always returns to the church for *pascha*, to the home with the Paschal Light. Women from other traditions must always recognize the limitations that face an Orthodox feminist who is seeking to effect changes in the church.

Women who are able to stay in Catholic, Protestant or Orthodox church structures although their calls for *metanoia* (repentance) and change are treated with hostility or benign neglect do so out of a commitment to truth and to the ecumenical vision of the church in unity. We have stated our claim to be church, as ones baptized and taking on Christ (Gal. 3:27). And even where we have gained authority and ordination and recognition of our ministries, we should not forget that all our churches have their own forms of patriarchal oppression and their own style of hierarchy — which even women have yearned to participate in.

All of us know women, often in our own parishes, who have faithfully committed their lives to the church and who consider what we write, say and do an offence within the church, totally contrary to scriptural admonitions concerning woman's behaviour and status. Many of these women have no experience of ecumenical friendship and are bound entirely to their own small part of the church. A growing number is joining fundamentalist movements within all traditions who raise critical voices about efforts to change the traditional role of women in church. They cannot be ignored.

Thus we should not suppose that the way we think and write and act is common among the women of the church. We are privileged women, with education, the ability to read and to discern, to learn and to teach, to travel and to be in dialogue with women of different races, churches, cultures and traditions. This privilege brings responsibility and discomfort, and at times misunderstanding and anger.

However, we must remember that such dialogue and open sharing illuminate the whole church, not just women. It is from such forums that we often move on to challenging the centuries of oppressive male structures in church and society, which have smothered our dissenting voices, ensured our submissiveness, enforced our self-guilt and separated us into the private sphere of subservient piety. Another voice from the nineteenth century, Matilda Gage, speaks to women in the church today:

> Woman will gain nothing by a compromising attitude toward the church, by attempts to excuse its great wrongs against her sex, or by palliation of its motives. On the contrary, a stern reference to facts, keeping the face of the world turned toward its past teachings and its present attitude is her duty. Wrongs of omission equal in magnitude those of commission.[9]

In many Orthodox communities there is virtually no knowledge of scholarly insights into the scriptures and the writings of the early church. Most people assume that what is, is as it always has been; and women do not raise questions, but continue the traditions of millennia. This is not to say that their life in the church is diminished or ignorant. Among those unconcerned by feminist issues are women of great piety and faithfulness, whose relationship with their God is totally giving. Rather than dismissing them, it is important to find ways to understand their journey. But it is regrettable that the hierarchs of the church too often look only to the women of obedience and service (who may grumble like Martha at the physical tasks before them) and ignore the challenge and excitement raised by the new voices of women who research, read and question, seldom fetch a cup of tea and in fact demand a place with Mary at the Teacher's feet (Luke 10:38-42) or with Photeine alongside him (John 4:3-30).

To be sure, in a few dioceses — in the USA and France, for instance — there are some women theological students and scholars. Nevertheless, the exclusion and lack of encouragement overall for women to be involved in extensive dialogue within the Orthodox Church, other than in very traditional ways for traditional purposes, only serves to confirm an image of a misogynist and patriarchal church, where women are seen and not heard.

New voices

For some years I have belonged to a rather unique group of women in the church: women committed to ecumenical dialogue, feminists seeking to find themselves and their history in the hidden stories and traditions of the church, women who stay in their church in order to affect change. We are convinced that the church is not meant to be frozen in the past, that within the church the Holy Spirit may still dwell freely among us, that prophetic voices may be heard from the least of us, "that in Christ there is neither male nor female" (Gal. 3:28) and that in our lives as believers in a transcendent, personal and yet unknowable God, we dwell on this earth as an image of that greatness and purity, seeking through our life's journey the kingdom of God.

Two women who have begun to focus feminist questions for Orthodox women are Eva Catafygiotu Topping from the USA and Elisabeth Behr-Sigel of France.

Eva Topping has been attacked, sometimes venomously, in church publications, but her work has been eagerly read by Orthodox women who have been exposed through it to a traditional feminine and hidden feminist tradition of the church. An Orthodox hymnographer, Greek and Latin scholar, she has uncovered much of the misogyny and deliberately anti-woman theology written and reinforced by successive fathers of the church. She has also portrayed feminist women of incredible strength and faith who defied emperors and patriarchs whose teaching they perceived as incorrect. In time, often after death, the women were acknowledged as correct in their theological interpretation and honourable in their pursuit of truth. Eva Topping's essays in *Holy Mothers of Orthodoxy* challenge the church, clergy and laity, to question its actions and attitudes towards women in community, society and liturgical practice.

Elisabeth Behr-Sigel is known in France for her considerable academic and theological contributions, and some of her writings have been translated into English. She has been fortunate in being part of an Orthodox community characterized by searching minds and challenging theological thought. She has offered the Orthodox church her theological insights on a variety of issues in many forums, and was the first to raise in recent times the question of ministry and ordination of women in the Orthodox Church. Her book *The Ministry of Women in the Orthodox Church* is a guide to the questions emerging, albeit slowly, from the Orthodox tradition. She has defended her findings with skill and "right knowledge":

> Can we say the Orthodox have nothing to receive from the Western women's movement...? Can we ignore and neglect the questions being asked of the churches today? Should we not be attentive to the "signs of the times" and to what the Spirit is saying to the churches in each generation?... Authentic faithfulness consists in building on the foundations...[10]

These two women are not young firebrands tarnished by the influence of the supposedly unruly voices of Western secular feminism. Rather they are women of mature years, faithful adherents of Orthodox tradition and liturgical life, who through their experience and scholarship have found questions that are right and essential at this time for the Orthodox Church. Becoming acquainted with the writings and work of many others is much more difficult. However, the network, while scattered, is growing, albeit differently from the Western feminist tradition.

One problem I have observed among Orthodox women is a deep sense that they need permission from a priest to meet and explore their own tradition with the questions of today. Even strong Orthodox women who are well educated in history, sociology and theology suppose that the priest's presence will offer legitimacy to a discussion and of course prevent false teaching. But the experience of the presence of men at some seminars originally planned for women has been that the ambience is altered and the questions are changed. Their presence silences women and prevents the journey of feminine and feminist beginning for most Orthodox women.

Of course this is not the whole story. In the USA, France, Greece, Russia and Finland, for instance, women have access to theological education at seminaries. They are involved in the full life of the parish and the full range of responsibilities of the laity. After university education, more and more women are entering monastic orders, which provide strong spiritual centres for women and men in their region. Likewise, the role of the priest's wife is increasingly being seen as a distinct vocation that women offer the church. In the USA, a network is growing of clergy wives, many of whom have graduate degrees in theology and wish to contribute their learning and ministry to the church. A new organization called WOMEN (Women's Orthodox Ministries and Education Network) should open up opportunities for dialogue among Orthodox women, and between them and Catholic and Protestant women in the USA.

Women and the liturgy

The liturgical life of the Orthodox carries a great richness and splendour in its music and icons, in the building itself and in the embroidered vestments of its clergy. It is a wondrous experience at Easter to behold the brilliance of the liturgy, and to be transported by the beauty of prayer. The feminine presence is obvious, though strangely quiet; the feminist presence non-existent. As in all other churches, the majority of worshippers are women. There are many icons of women saints. The Theotokos is present in the sanctuary and elsewhere to be venerated by the faithful.

Yet there are disturbing features for a feminist entering the church for liturgy. In many churches, women and men sit separately, often the women upstairs away from the men. The cantors are men, except on high days when women may sing in the choir, as are the readers who chant the psalms and prayers and read the epistle, those who process the icons and carry the candles. Their sons serve as altar boys.

So where are the women? They may be absent because they are menstruating. They are forbidden to enter the sanctuary, which is supposedly only for the priest or "those pure in body and soul", though laymen and boys often seem quite at home there when it is deemed necessary. Women are passive in the pews, for the responses to prayers are left to the chanters, but their voices can often be heard whispering the liturgy, which they know so well from decades of faithful attendance. Where I stand in my church I see the Theotokos with her embracing arms in the dome of the sanctuary, seen but not approached by women. She is the model put before women as the ideal: ever-virgin and mother. When I see the crucified Christ atop the iconostasis with the two faithful women at the foot of the cross, and the resurrection icon, in which Christ brings forth both Adam and Eve from death, I rejoice — and I wonder where our living presence is today. For many, it seems, the church still places women with Eve before the resurrection. We still carry her sin, for it is Eve who is perceived as having introduced death to the world. As Eva Topping writes, Eve was seen as "the agent of sin and death and Satan's ally, and was turned from woman into a malevolent power or curse".[11]

Especially during Holy Week, women are present in the church, but in my parish church it is only as attenders in the pews. Even the words of the Theotokos mourning her son on Holy Thursday evening are sung by men:

> Today the blameless Virgin saw Thee hung upon the Cross; she mourned within herself and was sorely pierced in her heart. She groaned in agony from the depth of her soul, exhausted by smiting upon her breast, hair dishevelled, she cried out, "Alas, My Divine Son! Alas! Light of the World!"

On Holy Friday, women remain in church to prepare the tomb, the young girls re-enact the myrrh-bearers and the *angelakia*, and women sing the lamentations (in the choir, led by men, of course). These women prepare their families to receive holy communion, prepare the home to receive the Holy Light and to share the table and bless it by singing *"Christos Anesti!"* — Christ is risen! This is a special time for women, for there is a feeling of actually being in control and directing the celebrations of the resurrection. It is a powerful and moving experience to carry home the Light, to light the paschal candle and rejoice when breaking the fast and singing the praises. At this time it seems that the church — that is, the "little church" — is whole and inclusive, as it was intended by Christ. Cleansed by fasting, fulfilled by communion and enriched by the liturgy, we are as one with all in the church.

Hope for change

The experience of a non-ethnic Orthodox woman living in the church in the diaspora is different from that of a woman living in Greece or

Russia, for example, where the church is the community. In the diaspora, there is a different perspective on tradition. For me, there is a close relationship with other churches through the ecumenical movement, as well as involvement in the Christian and secular feminist movement. Life experience and our place in community with each other cannot be ignored, for they shape our perceptions and demand reflection. They can either call us to God or turn our face away.

In Australia all our churches should be grappling with the dilemmas of its people moving into the new century. Regrettably, the National Commission on the Status of Women in the Church, a commission of the Australian Council of Churches, ceased its work for the churches at the end of June 1994 when the new National Council of Churches in Australia was created. So far, there is little evidence that the churches will ask a similar body to examine issues of profound importance to women in the church, even in relation to the Ecumenical Decade. The issues for all women in the church are the same. And to ignore the voices and the concerns of Orthodox women, both secular and theological issues, will be to the detriment of the life of the whole church.

John Erikson has written that "the Orthodox woman must avoid the temptation to consider the church only in static, a-temporal and other-worldly terms and take seriously the challenges posed by historical change".[12] If the Holy Spirit is indeed free in our time, then the church will not and cannot prevent change as challenges arise from among the faithful believers. Tradition does not make us prisoners of our past; rather, it reveals the Spirit at work in both past and present.[13] Opportunities for dialogue between women of faith will always bring forth new challenges, create more questions, and enlighten the church universal.

Orthodox women are blessed with the great richness of liturgical life of our church, life that very naturally spills into the home. One is always aware of the relationship and meaning of "the liturgy after the liturgy". I cannot imagine this changing. What I desire is the inclusion of women in liturgical practice wherever laity are involved, not in a special role, but in one that is natural in the order of the church. The issue of the ordination of women to the diaconate and the priesthood is "on the agenda". Though at this stage no woman or group is prepared to devote their life to the cause, the church has acknowledged the need for discussion and theological reflection.

Whether the decades ahead will bring the changes experienced in other denominations I cannot judge. The issues raised by Orthodox women concerning our role and participation in the life of the church, expressed in moderate, conservative language, must be taken seriously by the hierarchs and clergy and men of the church. Culture and tradition must not be kept in place by the iron bands of history and ignorance in the name of church doctrine.

Women in all Orthodox jurisdictions must take seriously the challenges before them, refusing to be forced to choose between secular and spiritual within their community. Whether in the diaspora or "at home", the feminist challenge is present in the Orthodox churches, albeit on the edges, muted, isolated and often vilified. We take examples from the women friends of Christ and from the women of the early church with their discipleship, preaching and evangelical work. We seek to emulate women of leadership, the martyrs, ascetics and monastics. We have a heritage of women worthy of recognition. If we are to be the church of true faith and right practice, which the Orthodox Church claims to be, then only the inclusion of women as equal members of the "royal priesthood" in all its many facets will truly make it so.

For proceeding to such an ideal of fully inclusive participation, feminist theology with its demand for the hermeneutics of suspicion, critical analysis of hierarchy and patriarchy and revelation of the hidden women of church history and scripture can only be a positive, liberating influence on women seeking to understand and to challenge existing structures, contemporary theological understandings and the exclusive cultural traditions that are demeaning and exclusive to women in the Orthodox Church.

NOTES

[1] Timothy Ware, *The Orthodox Church*, Harmondsworth, UK, Penguin, 1969, p.205.

[2] *Ibid.*, p.203.

[3] Elisabeth Schüssler Fiorenza, *In Memory of Her*, London, SCM, 1983, p.176.

[4] Elisabeth Schüssler Fiorenza, "Breaking the Silence — Becoming Visible", in *Concilium*, No.182, December 1985, p.7.

[5] *Shafts*, Vol. 1, No. 1, 3 November 1892, p.19.

[6] Quoted by Eva Topping, *Saints and Sisterhood*, Minneapolis, Life & Light, 1990, p.141.

[7] Eva C. Topping, *Holy Mothers of Orthodoxy*, Minneapolis, Life & Light, 1987, p.121.

[8] *Saints and Sisterhood*, pp.vii-viii.

[9] Matilda Joslyn Gage, *Woman, Church and State*, orig. ed. 1900, repr. Salem, NH, Ayer, 1992, p.542.

[10] Elisabeth Behr-Sigel, *The Ministry of Women in the Church*, Torrance, CA, Oakwood Publishing Co., 1991, p.123.

[11] *Holy Mothers of Orthodoxy*, p.64.

[12] John Erikson, *The Challenge of Our Past*, Crestwood NY, St Vladimir's Seminary Press, 1991, p.5.

[13] *Ibid.*, p.7.

Seeking Dialogue with the Church: Christian Women in the Middle East

MARY MIKHAEL

We live in a world and a church where women are speaking with a new voice and new urgency. Since the Nairobi conference in 1985 which marked the close of the UN Decade for Women, much has been said and done with regard to women's issues. In September 1995 Beijing will host a fourth UN world conference on women. This global forum will assess what has been achieved since Nairobi to bring out women's strengths, skills and talents and to move towards a global policy of gender equality, development and peace.

At Easter 1988 the World Council of Churches launched the Ecumenical Decade of Churches in Solidarity with Women, 1988-1998. Now at the midpoint of the Decade, churches in the Middle East seem far from being involved, despite the fact that women are quite vocal in openly raising its objectives. The Decade continues to be seen as an outside idea on which one should not rush to comment.

However, living in Beirut one can observe exhilarating activities on the part of several women's groups: the Lebanese Women's Council, the Human Rights Movement, the Institute of Women's Studies and others. They are calling for equal opportunities for women in education, training and participation in decision-making processes. There was special interest in women's issues within the Catholic family during 1994, with preparations for the Synod for Lebanon. Special seminars have been held, television programmes have interviewed leading women, the newspaper *Biblia* published a special issue on women, books and articles and workshops have marked a special and genuine concern in regard to women's rights.

This paper seeks to be a humble contribution and a sincere participation on this journey with women here in Lebanon and everywhere else in the world, even though I may look at women's issues from a different angle from those of my Lebanese sisters mentioned above. I approach the subject as a Christian woman who finds her identity only in sharing with the church its vision and its mission.

Partnership and patriarchy

When reading the book of Genesis we find that it is a fact of creation that men and women are partners. The partnership of women and men is God's intention for humanity. The Genesis story goes on to tell us that men and women have fallen short of God's expectations and were cut off from their intimate relationship with God. Eve, the woman, was an agent in the fall which caused a curse upon humanity and nature. The woman's share in that curse was an increased pain in childbirth and man's rule over her.

Thus as a result of the events portrayed in the early chapters of the book of Genesis, women in the biblical tradition are subordinate to men and looked upon as the proximate cause of the fall into sin. Coupled with the social system, this created the patriarchal system so evident in the whole of the Old Testament. The picture of society manifested in the Old Testament introduces man as predominant and women as subordinate and places in man's hands the policy-making for life and conduct on every level. Woman is weaker and expected to execute decisions and policies made entirely by man. Her humanity is thus shaped by man. Her identity is drawn from her relationship to man — husband, father or brother, as the case may be. Patriarchy as a system is presented as the will of God, unquestioned and undebated. Men are rulers over women in matters of religion and society. Woman's status is that of a follower; and quite often a woman seems to be no more than a man's property, especially because man has the monopoly of religion. In this respect, the women's image in the Old Testament corresponds exactly to the image of women in Middle Eastern society even in the 20th century.

Margaret B. Crook traces man's monopoly of religion to Miriam's indignant question: "Has the Lord spoken only through Moses?" (Num. 12:2). Since then, men have formulated doctrines and established systems of religion and worship that offer only meagre opportunity for woman-kind to express its religious genius. Miriam then was shamefully struck with leprosy. Today such leprosy shows itself in countless forms of violence against women.

So in many different ways the patriarchal system present in the image of society in both the Old Testament and our own day has itself shaped the image of woman and framed her in a frame of man's own imagination and desire.

Notice that man's rule over woman was part of the curse, which is the result of sin, a state of being that came out of negating the will of God. This has become the norm in society, socially as well as religiously. In the process of daily life this social norm has created much oppression and often violence against women. Women have been systematically marginalized and excluded from writing history, from creating philosophy, science and law.

Women in the Middle East have more often than not been denied equal opportunities with men in education and training, in career advancement, in realizing a free and independent way of life. And although women are the majority in most services, they are structured into social institutions as though they were the minority.

In order to legitimize patriarchy as a divine system, our society, like the Old Testament, presents God in terms that give a strongly masculine impression. Typical passages speak of God as king, judge, mighty warrior and other similar images. And despite feminine images of God found in the Old Testament, the language used there for God is totally that which is typical for addressing a man. Phyllis Trible notes that Hebrew grammar uses masculine pronouns for God, and although grammatical gender determines neither sexuality nor theology, these masculine pronouns reinforce a male image of God and obscure or obliterate female metaphors for deity.

To address God as male is to frame or limit God to our own categories and purposes. Language influences the way we think and act and is in turn shaped by the culture of the speaker. According to Robert Hamerton-Kelly, Jesus' use of the familiar term "Abba" for God was intended to emphasize the freedom and love of the new family of God's reign in opposition to the existing patriarchal family structure. Sallie McFague suggests that the problem is not that God is imaged as Father but that we have made Father as God. Of course, every name we use for God is partial — God transcends male images, female images and every other image or God would not be God. With every name we use for God we are also describing ourselves and the relationships that exist between ourselves and God. In naming God we are able to find our identity within God, God within our own identity. Thus, when the church uses exclusively the masculine gender for God and addresses God as a male, and then goes on to refer to the whole community in similar terms — for example, "brothers in the faith" — women are excluded from being in relationship with God. This contradicts the truth and realities of women in God.

As Lavinia Byrne says in *Women Before God*, "When the language offered for our use in church fails to name women, it excludes me and most of what I do. It allows me neither to celebrate my own identity nor to reflect upon the place of God in my experience." Male exclusive language in the Bible and in worship excludes woman from participation; inclusive language builds up a community of partners.

It is by all means true that the Bible maintains an authority for life and faith. However, the Bible has been one of the most important means by which women's place in society has been defined. And throughout the centuries the Bible has been invoked to justify women's subordination to men. Yet the Bible has also played a sometimes surprising role in empowering women.

Concerning patriarchy, for example, notice that every now and then the text modestly surprises us with a woman who breaks out of the frame and becomes a free soul. Miriam, for example, openly punished and publicly silenced in the book of Numbers because she asked whether God spoke only through Moses, is quietly reconsidered by God himself in Micah 6:4: "For I brought you up from the land of Egypt, and redeemed you from the house of bondage: and I sent before you Moses, Aaron and Miriam." Deborah, a mother in Israel just as Abraham was a father in Israel, governed the nation as a judge exactly like Samuel. Later, Huldah was the only one who could discern the word of God and interpret the law to renew and reform the religious life of the nation.

Moses himself, the great liberator of his people, was the product of a host of women who defied and manipulated the system. Two professional women (midwives) saved his life, his mother and sister protected and educated him in religion, an unmarried young woman, Pharaoh's daughter, brought him up in the highest civilization and scientific achievement of the time. Later his wife protected and supported him in his liberating mission. Each of these women acted against the system in her own way.

Several other women have left their imprint on the pages of the Old Testament, exhibiting wisdom far beyond the men to whom they were related — Abigail, Ruth, the mother of Lemuel, even Rahab and Jezebel. Although these and other outstanding women are few in number, I believe this is clear enough evidence that even the Old Testament record contains a critique of total patriarchy if one is a careful reader.

Jesus, Paul and the church

On the surface the New Testament does not seem to bring much change in these matters. Despite Jesus' open challenge, critique and sometimes rejection of existing social norms, the new community, the church, has emerged as a male-dominated society, although Jesus Christ preached good news to the poor, proclaimed release to the captives, recovery of sight to the blind and liberty for the oppressed. And despite the fact that the message of the New Testament is that of mending and renewing the old creation — "everything old has passed away" (2 Cor. 5:17) — some contrary social norms have hung on in the church, dictating women's conduct and defining their roles and ministry.

In the movement of Jesus and the life of the early church, women did gain many rights. Women enjoyed forgiveness, healing and restoration of mind, body and social status. In the company of Jesus, they were able to stand on the same ground as men. They were taught by Jesus as well as sent by him. They were praised for their interest in his teaching and rebuked when they complained. Women served Jesus, went around with him, hosted the church in their own homes. Women were even dragged to prisons alongside men for their faith in Jesus Christ.

The gospels do not record any discrimination against women. On the contrary, when one examines the gospel of Luke, one notices a special interest in women, in the lowly and outcast, in the oppressed and all those who were classified by the social system as unworthy. Luke portrays Mary the mother of Jesus as one of radical faith and radical courage. "Let it be with me according to your word" (Luke 1:38) was her response to the angel who told her she would be the mother of the one who would be called Emmanuel, "God with us". Luke shows in unique ways that women display primacy over men in the area of love and faith.

With the spread of Christianity to wider geographical areas the place of women seems to have shrunk behind a veil. How often we hear opponents of women in church leadership saying, "If Jesus wanted women to serve in the church he would have included a woman among the twelve apostles." It is true that there is no record of the inclusion of women among the twelve apostles, but so what? It was women who first met the risen Lord, and they were sent to the disciples with the dazzling news that Jesus is risen. And if the number twelve was so significant, why did one drop out and we never again hear of the one who replaced him? On the other hand, one may note that the New Testament never addresses the issue of slavery. Are we to assume that it should continue and be accepted as the will of God?

The early church had a lot of courage to oppose social and political and religious authorities and to declare at the risk of death that God has acted in Christ on behalf of the oppressed and powerless and the marginalized. However, for reasons unknown to us, the church maintained rules and practices that have kept women in the shadow of men. Feminist theologians relate this to the struggle for authority and power in the church. Thus for centuries women were denied opportunity to participate in decision-making processes in the church and to hold any leading positions.

John writes that Jesus came to his own home, and his own people did not receive him, but that all who received him, who believed in his name, were given power to become children of God (John 1:11-12). Here there is no discrimination of gift based on the sex of the believer.

Paul, who wrote on the one hand that women should keep silent in the church and be submissive in their learning, has also declared the Christian manifesto: "As many of you as were baptized into Christ have clothed yourselves with Christ. There is no longer Jew or Greek, there is no longer slave or free, there is no longer male and female; for all of you are one in Christ Jesus" (Gal. 3:27). Although he said to Timothy, "I do not allow a woman to teach", he never hesitated to teach with a woman partner in Corinth (Priscilla). Although he said that a woman should not have authority over a man because Eve was tempted, he did not give a second thought to whether a woman could be left in charge of the newly established Christian community in Philippi. Paul's message was in fact that of newness, of freedom in Christ — freedom from the power of the oppressors, freedom to be and to do, but to do all things decently and in proper order.

Bit by bit, the church has forgotten some parts of Paul and adhered strictly to others, in the process making Paul sound as if he were a misogynist. Was he so? The more serious question is: Was what God has done in Jesus Christ enough to mend the old creation and abolish the curse of the old fall? If not, then Jesus has died in vain.

So are the feminist theologians right in believing that the social norms that subordinate women in the church are related to the question of authority and power struggle? If not, how can we understand that a church father could say: "Woman! you are the devil's doorway. You have led astray one whom the devil would not dare attack directly. It is your fault that the Son of God had to die; you should always go in mourning and rags" (Tertullian)? How could Thomas Aquinas have said: "Woman is an occasional and incomplete being, a misbegotten male. It is unchangeable that woman is destined to live under man's influence and has not authority from her Lord... The image of God is found in the man, not the woman, for man is the beginning and end of woman"? If this is not related to authority and power and thus to patriarchy as a system, then I can hardly understand our much respected church fathers. Lavinia Byrne has said that "the problem for women is that the Christian tradition has been less open to human differences than the gospels are; the tradition has thought it necessary to set up one half of the human family at the expense of the other". This is, I believe, put mildly.

And so the patriarchal system in the church has prevailed for the last two thousand years. It is considered the will and plan of God that woman shall not participate in leadership positions, that power and authority shall be entirely in the hands of men.

A vision for the future

What should women do? Continue for another two thousand years? Maybe women will continue. But should the Christian church, men and women, not rather re-evaluate, analyze and critique patriarchy? If not, we endanger two fundamental values of our faith, justice and freedom. On the biblical view, justice is always justice for *all*. Justice is God's option in favour of those suffering from injustice, the weak and the powerless. At the same time, the Bible is a great book about liberation. If one person is not free then all are not free. But what if half of the human family is not free?

Patriarchy in the Bible subtly hides the elements of domination and dependence which are contrary to the liberating purpose of God's intervention in history. Domination of men over women belongs to those fundamental assumptions which are never questioned or seen as problems because they have been part of the social contract which has defined the roles, division of labour and allocation of power between men and women. This hardly matches the message of liberation brought by Jesus Christ.

Of course things are changing. Many men and women around the world have begun to evaluate, analyze and critique the patriarchal system, and as a result new things are emerging. In some churches in some parts of the world some women have regained the opportunity to participate in the service of the church as equals to men, including ordination to the ministry and in a few cases as bishops. These changes have not come without much pain, and the ordination of women has now become a decisive point for the continuation or termination of ecumenical dialogue.

Where do women of the Middle Eastern churches stand? What should be our attitude as Oriental women and churches? What is our vision for the future? Should we separate ourselves from the struggle of women in the world? Should we disregard women's issues as a foreign transplant that cannot survive in our soil and thus go on as if nothing is the matter? Women's issues related to justice and freedom, human rights, religion and faith are indeed our own issues; and we are deeply concerned about what happens to women here and around the world. We are concerned that oppression and violence against women be eliminated. We are concerned that women of skills, talents and gifts have room to use these. What is our stand and what should we do? Revolt? Yes and No. Yes, we revolt against violence, oppression and deprivation of the opportunity to be and to do. No, we shall not revolt against the church, for there we shall lose anyway. But we wish in humility, faith and love to enter into dialogue with the church. We want along with the church to analyze, examine and critique the prevailing systems. We want to rediscover the liberating elements in the Bible.

Our vision for the future is the old vision from the past as it renews itself continuously, the vision of an amended creation, the new creation in the vision and mission of Christ. Our vision is that of the future of God who intended that men and women live in partnership, in *koinonia*. This partnership, according to Letty M. Russell, "is a new focus of relationship in a common history of Jesus Christ that sets persons free for others". This partnership with Christ is a two-sided relationship of giving and receiving, participation and impartation. "It is a form of partnership rooted in the life story of Jesus Christ, yet containing small anticipations of God's intended partnership of new creation." Did not God himself enter into partnership with humanity? "Do we not find our archetype of partnership within God in the persons of the Holy Trinity? Do we not find in the Holy Trinity an image of mutuality, reciprocity and a totally shared life?" Such a vision of partnership will help to create a more truly human society and church where justice, liberation and hope will constitute our lives and relationships.

Will the church of the Middle East accept to dialogue with us? Will it share with us our vision?

Feminist Theology:
A View from the Pacific

MARIE ROPETI

This paper cannot of course represent the voices of all women in the context where I live, but will reflect on some of the work on women's analysis taking place in my part of the Pacific.

I am a Samoan living permanently in Aotearoa New Zealand. I am a Presbyterian minister teaching Pacific studies at the University of Otago and Knox Theological Hall. Part of my work is to provide the Presbyterian Church with resources related to issues concerning the Pacific islands.

Growing up in Samoa, I experienced the lack of participation of women in the leadership and decision-making of the church. Women were and still are pastors' wives and wives of elders. My father was a pastor of the Congregational Christian Church in Samoa (begun by the London Missionary Society). Within the home, he was the leader of family devotions and decision-making — the first to consult about any changes in the family. His ministry was the source of our lives as a family. The whole issue of women's role in leadership did not bother us much until I decided to become a pastor. My father, knowing the rules of the church, was reluctantly supportive, but my mother was a forerunner who was by my side to ensure that my goal was fulfilled.

In 1974 the elder pastors of my church were challenged to face the issue of women studying in the theological college when a young woman showed interest in attending. The outcome of their discussion was: "Our church is not ready for this change, but maybe she can be trained overseas." Twenty years later, despite the voices of many Pacific women who have attended World Council of Churches' women's meetings, a discussion of women in ministry by the South Pacific Association of Theological Schools in 1989 and a good deal of work done by women in the church, my home church, like many other Protestant churches in the Pacific, is still "not ready for this change".

I moved to Aotearoa New Zealand mainly to pursue what I believed was a call to ministry in the church. In 1975 Presbyterian women there were celebrating the tenth anniversary of the first ordination of a woman to ministry. My contacts were with the Presbyterian Church of Aotearoa New Zealand, whose membership includes large groups of Pacific islanders and Maoris, and my own feminist awareness was increased as I studied at the University of Otago and at Knox Theological Hall.

Women in the Presbyterian Church of Aotearoa New Zealand

Generally, women had a very traditional, supportive role in the Presbyterian Church, and the system of education for church employment reinforced this. Once separate training for men and women was abolished in 1970, however, the expectations of women for opportunities to minister changed. (A valuable resource on this history is *Women of Burning Bush*, the report of a survey of women ministers in the Presbyterian Church of Aotearoa New Zealand after 25 years of ordination.)

But even if the structures now allow women into the ordained ministry, the attitudes among both ordained and lay people about who women are and what they can do have not changed to the same extent. Discrimination because of sex is still a matter for debate, and women's equality is still open to question. The general assembly decided in 1986 not to licence a male minister because he refused to take part in the ordination of women, but the fact that this case took two years to resolve indicates that there is not yet a clear universal acceptance of women's equality.

An increasing number of women are going into Knox Theological Hall with more critical eyes than their mothers'. Only very recently are a few women doing professional theology from women's perspective, and only one course is offered at the Hall which specifically introduces questions of feminist interpretation.

Historically, women have been seen as second-class members in the church; and as a result they often believed that they were not good enough for leadership in ministry. It was not that they lacked the necessary qualities and skills, but that they did not have the confidence to affirm themselves. Consequently, some women in ministry are surprised at what they are able to accomplish personally and what has been accomplished within the church so far, and are prepared to continue slowly. Others, however, are saying, "We can't wait any longer. We have the authority of God and want to get on with the job on equal terms." This latter group see that they could easily be boxed into a feminized trap which people are comfortable with. It is much easier to survive by acquiescing to the stereotypical model and focusing on pastoral skills than by working to develop a critical philosophy of faith and theology. The temptation for women is to be domesticated rather than to be prophetic or scholarly in ways that are strong.

The ordained women have a personal knowledge and experience of the empowering joy of knowing God, and they want to share this with the people of Aotearoa New Zealand. They are committed to removing quickly any practices within the Presbyterian Church which put barriers in the way of women. They do not want to be divisive or different. They do not want to be female against male or female against female. What they want is acceptance, freedom and equality, a climate in which gender is not an issue and the focus is on developing the best ways to provide ministry for all people, including each other.

In 1992 a group of women moved that the general assembly receive their report, calling for serious consideration of its implementation in the whole church. Part of the report includes this commitment: "The Presbyterian Church of Aotearoa New Zealand has one ministry: male and female, and from any ethnic origin. All are equal. Equality, though, does not just happen. It has to be made to happen and it calls for constant vigilance."

Pacific women in Aotearoa New Zealand

Within the Pacific islander section of the Presbyterian and Methodist churches in Aotearoa New Zealand, the idea of women in ministry has had very limited impact. A few Pacific island women are ministers, and for these pioneers of change there are always risks involved: the risk of having our abilities and potentials undermined, the risk of constantly being compared with men and having all that we say or do criticized. But over against this we have experienced the strength of support provided by our sisters who have gone before us in ministry.

Pacific island women in the churches of Aotearoa New Zealand suffer a double oppression. Pacific island communities in Aotearoa New Zealand are led mainly by men. Most of the Pacific island women ministers at the Theological Hall entered with the support of a white congregation because their own Pacific island parish would not support them. When we fight for justice and equity for women we are often seen as "white feminist". When we fight for justice and equity on racial issues we are often viewed as "one of the island boys".

The reality is that a Pacific island parish will not call a woman to be its minister for reasons of cultural sensitivity. With male-dominated ministers informing the people about the role of women on the basis of their biblical interpretations, the issue of women has never been discussed properly among Pacific island people.

Sexism is not an excuse to avoid addressing racism. Often the church fails to recognize that women of other cultures have struggles which are unique to their own context. In the process of trying to legitimate their own position in the church, some women ministers unconsciously adopt male attitudes and exclusive and patronizing ways. This makes it all too easy to accept church policies which actually discriminate against women. Practically, when men are present in church meetings, Pacific women tend to remain silent. The patriarchal social structure in many Pacific congregations spells out the superiority of males and the inferiority of females. This way of life is strengthened by the churches' conservative interpretation of biblical passages concerning the place and status of women.

I see this oppression of women as a challenge to women theologians around the world. Our task is to find ways to liberate the leaders of the church as well as the women who feel excluded.

My own involvement in the work of the church has blessed me with the knowledge that women are gifted in so many ways different from men. And when these gifts are allowed to be shared in the church for ministry, we will have a more harmonious, peaceful church which embraces all its members equally.

While Pacific people in the Methodist and Presbyterian churches in Aotearoa New Zealand accept women in ministry, the long-range concern for a more inclusive ministry must grow out of our island churches themselves, where women are not yet accepted as ministers. Pacific island people in Aotearoa New Zealand retain a strong cultural bond to their island churches. While the island churches close the doors on women ministers for reasons of culture, they can be challenged by a more open feminist interpretation of the gospel in relation to sexuality, culture and the Bible.

During the last ten years or so there has been a growing tendency among Pacific women to involve themselves in many activities in which they are not really recognized. They use their capacities and talents not only in the social area, to which they were previously confined, but also in decision-making positions. Some of them have even succeeded in gaining important positions in the political and religious spheres. This has led to strong reactions not only from men, for they feel invaded by women, but also from other women. Some say that the women's movement is an idea foreign to the Pacific which has been introduced to destabilize the traditional way of life in the Pacific.

I believe that many Pacific women who want to be more involved in church decision-making and leadership have been enlightened by what they have discovered in studying how the word of God speaks to them in their lives. They have experienced the love of God in a very inclusive way. This love has given them values and potential through which they can bring about changes, whether in a quiet manner or in a more revolutionary way. They have questioned and broken some of the taboos by which their traditions and culture have confined them.

Culture and the teachings of certain churches continue to be used to keep women silent and prevent them from taking part in the whole life of the church. In the past when new ideas developed, many women were afraid of change for fear of being humiliated, while others have found themselves quite at ease with the status quo and do not hesitate to stop any move towards change instigated by other women.

Sisters from all parts of the world share their struggle as women. We are all on the same journey, though some of us are ahead of others. Looking to the ones before us, we learn from their rise and fall and their openness. Looking to the ones behind us, we are encouraged by their strength and hope.

We as Pacific women are challenged to question our traditions, those values and teachings which have been established by the church and prevent us from contributing fully in the life of our church as leaders. When we face problems, we know we are not alone; we shall turn to our sisters from other parts of the world and make a connection. I believe that when we are bound together in our struggle we become stronger to face whatever comes our way.

Women in Dialogue: Wholeness of Vision towards the 21st Century

The Message from the Bossey Seminar

We have gathered as women to envision a just future in church and society, for women, for children and for men. Much threatens such a future. To create it will be hard work. For the majority of women on earth, this is first of all the hard work of survival.

We have gathered to begin envisioning the 21st century,
 by letting the light of our lives' stories shine,
  even with the fires of tribulation;
 by celebrating our diversity and honouring our differences,
  even when they lead to conflict; and
 by committing ourselves to act together for a just future,
  even when we are divided by economic, political,
  cultural, and religious structures and beliefs.

We are united
 by our solemn rejection of the pervasive, growing
  violence against women in the whole world;
 by our hope in the freedom born of faith
  in Mary's son, Jesus; and
 by our desire for a new, whole community of human beings,
  earth and all creatures, within the embrace of God.

We have had a foretaste of the church of the future in our daily worship together. Celebration, local diversity, local ways of prayer and music, mutual conversation about Scripture — in meditation and praise we were one community embodied in our diversity and worshipping God, the Source of Life.

We are women from islands and all continents, from 33 countries. We are young and more aged women. We are members of churches in Anglican, Roman Catholic, Orthodox and Protestant communions. We do our daily work in many ways: as spiritual directors, teachers, mothers, priests, professors of theology, activists for women's rights, journalists and many other ministries of daily life. We have been gathered by the Ecumenical Institute at Bossey and the women's programmes of the World Council of Churches, the World Alliance of Reformed Churches, the Lutheran World Federation and the Conference of European Churches. We have been inspired by hearing stories of women's struggles for justice in church and society. The struggles for food, health, education, political freedom, work, bodily integrity have been women's lot for thousands of years. We envision a future in which survival is not an impossible hope for millions of human beings.

We search the Bible and our traditions for signs of hope and resources for change to envision the 21st century as a new millennium of well-being for women, children and men. We have heard reports on the progress and struggles of women in the Caribbean, Australia, Latin America, Africa, Asia, Europe, North America and the Pacific region. In our conversations we realized the need to call women's action and reflection as Christians by a variety of names. This theology is womanist for African American women. It is women's liberation theology for many in Latin America and Africa. For others it is feminist theology. Latinas in the United States call it *mujerista* theology. For Orthodox women, some call themselves feminist, while others are women reflecting on the theological tradition of Orthodoxy. For many women theology is the action and reflection on work in popular movements. Whatever the name, we are all creating women's reflection on and committed action with God in the world. By whatever name, we are women who commit ourselves to the daily struggle for the survival and well-being of those who live in the world as female human beings and for a just world for all people and other creatures.

In theological reflecting we discover long-hidden aspects of scripture and tradition which empower us, and we reject long-highlighted aspects which degrade us as women. We rejoice in theology which celebrates our female embodied selves as good creation. We reject theology which ignores or defends suffering which is imposed on us and models of sacrifice which reinforce violence in family, community and nations.

We brought our communities to the conference — in language, social customs, histories, etc. We were often enriched by each other's experience. However, we also experienced the agony of racism in our conference, as the global culture of whiteness overwhelms other cultures, peoples and individuals. Repenting of racism is essential for those who benefit from it; conversion to the struggle against racism and restitution are required for reconciliation with those who are harmed by it.

In the churches more and more women are engaging in theological interpretation of sexuality. We envision a future in which sexuality and violence will no longer be linked. Incest, rape and battering will be no more. Sexual harassment and male privilege will be over. Customs and rituals which endanger the health and rights of women will be eliminated. Violence against lesbians and gay men will be no more. Prostitution and sex tourism will have disappeared. The sexual abuse of children will be no more. The abuse of power through sexuality will be absent from clergy, counsellors and all professionals. Economic necessity will no longer compel women to sell themselves nor to be sold. Marriage will be a mutual, equal, free commitment for those who choose it or receive it as a gift from God. Women will be honoured, whether single, in relationship, married, divorced, widowed, in religious orders, mothers, yearning to be mothers. All women will be honoured and appropriately supported in public policy, economic structures, cultural values and theology. Incarnation as sexual beings (men and women) will be celebrated with delight and dignity.

We confess that some of us benefit from local, national and global structures which sap the life-blood from gasping peoples, especially women and children. Governments are pressured to "adjust" structures of society to meet requirements of international organizations which control the economic resources of the world. Traditional programmes for social welfare are replaced by privatization and market competition for resources required to meet basic human needs. This inevitably results in the exclusion of millions of children and women and men from access to adequate health services, food, education, transportation and possibilities of life-sustaining work. Such policies also wreak havoc with local and global environments and endanger the survival of the complex organism called Earth.

Halfway through the Ecumenical Decade of the Churches in Solidarity with Women, we call on the churches to join us in envisioning and acting for a new century. We call on the churches to:

— place women's survival and well-being at the centre of their programmes for social justice;
— give women access to all decision-making power in the church and further this access in society, working with women to exercise power in non-abusive, non-dominating ways;

— engage in dialogue and critical analysis of the economic, cultural and political context of each church's life and take appropriate action to combat injustice and to affirm life-giving elements in this context;
— work to eradicate the abuse of power and sexuality within the church, especially by clergymen and other church professionals;
— urge each other and especially the churches in Eastern Europe to participate fully in the Ecumenical Decade;
— reject violence as a solution to ethnic, political or religious differences, especially in the former Yugoslavia, Rwanda and wherever religions have been used or misused to fan the flames of hatred; and
— review the ongoing theological reflection and action of the churches to eliminate teaching and structures which prevent women from living the full meaning of our baptismal equality.

We know that in our hearts, minds, bodies that in these calls to our brothers and sisters, nothing less than the survival of millions of girls and boys, women and men is at stake. The promise of abundant life for all is our concrete hope for the 21st century. The struggle to realize this hope is the action through which we aspire to live our faith.

Contributors

Elizabeth Amoah (Methodist) is senior lecturer in the department for the study of religions at the University of Ghana, Accra.

Marguérite Fassinou is president of the Union of Methodist Women of Benin. She is a member of the WCC Commission on Faith and Order.

Musimbi Kanyoro from Kenya is secretary for women in church and society of the department for mission and development, Lutheran World Federation, Geneva.

Mary-John Mananzan from the Philippines (Roman Catholic) is coordinator of the women's programme of the Ecumenical Association of Third World Theologians, and chairperson of the women's movement "Gabriela".

Sun Ai Lee-Park (Disciples of Christ) is coordinator of the Asian Women's Resource Centre for Culture and Theology in Seoul, Korea, and editor of *In God's Image*.

Marlene Perera from Sri Lanka (Roman Catholic) is Asian coordinator for the Ecumenical Association of Third World Theologians.

Isabelle Graesslé (Reformed) is director of the Protestant study centre in Geneva, Switzerland.

Rosanna Panizo (Methodist) is director of the Biblical Theological Community in Lima, Peru.

Rosângela Soares de Oliveira (Methodist) is an advisor to the Sophia project of the Institute of Religious Studies in Rio de Janeiro, Brazil.

Elsa Tamez (Methodist) is director of the Latin American Biblical Seminary in San José, Costa Rica.

Elizabeth Bettenhausen (Lutheran) is director of studies at the Women's Theological Center in Boston, USA.

Letty M. Russell (Presbyterian) is professor of systematic theology at Yale University Divinity School, USA.

Delores S. Williams (Presbyterian) is associate professor of theology and culture at Union Theological Seminary, New York, USA.

Dorcas Gordon (Presbyterian) is director of the doctor of ministry programme at Toronto School of Theology, Canada.

Carol J. Schlueter teaches homiletics and pastoral theology at Waterloo Lutheran Seminary, Canada.

Leonie B. Liveris (Greek Orthodox), an historian, is editor of the international Orthodox women's journal *MaryMartha*. She lives in Perth, Australia.

Mary Mikhael (Presbyterian) is academic dean of the Near East School of Theology, Beirut, Lebanon, and director of the women's programme of the Middle East Council of Churches.

Marie Ropeti, a Presbyterian minister, teaches Pacific studies at Knox Theological Hall, Dunedin, Aotearoa, New Zealand.